Merry Christmas Rod & Meredith! from Todd & Melissa

Merry Christmas Rod & Meredith! from Todd & Melissa

This Book Belongs To
Meredith Bleifun

Seed
Leaf
Flower
Fruit

Maryjo Koch

SWANS ISLAND BOOKS

SMITHMARK

THIS EDITION PUBLISHED IN 1998 BY SMITHMARK PUBLISHERS, A DIVISION OF U.S. MEDIA HOLDINGS, INC.,
115 WEST 18TH STREET, NEW YORK, NY 10011.

SMITHMARK BOOKS ARE AVAILABLE FOR BULK PURCHASE FOR SALES PROMOTION AND PREMIUM USE. FOR
DETAILS WRITE OR CALL THE MANAGER OF SPECIAL SALES, SMITHMARK PUBLISHERS, 115 WEST 18TH STREET,
NEW YORK, NY 10011; (212) 519-1300.

PUBLISHED IN 1995 BY COLLINS PUBLISHERS SAN FRANCISCO, 1160 BATTERY STREET, SAN FRANCISCO, CA 94111

A SWANS ISLAND BOOK

LIBRARY OF CONGRESS CATALOG CARD NUMBER: 98-60011

ISBN 0-7651-0763-5

PRINTED IN HONG KONG
10 9 8 7 6 5 4 3 2 1

In memory of my mother
Freda

Seed

"A fairy seed I planted,
so dry and white and old,
there sprang a vine enchanted,
with magic flowers of gold."

—MARJORIE BARROWS, 1937

The eternal presence, beauty and variety of plants provide humankind with clues about the mysteries and meanings of life.

IN NEARLY EVERY RELIGION AND COSMOLOGY, PARADISE OR HEAVEN IS DESCRIBED AS A GARDEN. OUR ANCESTORS, WHO WORKED THE LAND, KNEW THAT PLANTS SUSTAIN NOT ONLY THE BODY, BUT THE MIND AND SPIRIT. THEY UNDERSTOOD THE LINKS BETWEEN PLANTS, MEDICINE, FOOD, SHELTER, AND THE GODS.

THREE THOUSAND YEARS BEFORE THE BIRTH OF CHRIST, EGYPTIANS WORSHIPPED THE LOTUS, OR NILE WATER LILY, A SYMBOL OF WOMEN, FERTILITY, AND IMMORTALITY.

WREATHS OF FRAGRANT LAUREL, THE PLANT OF THE GREEK GOD APOLLO, CROWNED POETS, ATHLETES, AND HEROES WITH HONOR. DIONYSUS AND BACCHUS CLAIMED IVY AS THE PLANT OF INSPIRATION AND ECSTASY.

A SYMBOL OF LIFE'S CONTINUITY THROUGH WINTER, THE EVERGREEN HOLLY DECORATES CHRISTMAS CELEBRATIONS. IN SPRING, WHITE LILIES SIGNIFY THE PURITY OF THE VIRGIN MARY, WHOSE MONTH IS MAY.

To keep fairies from entering their homes, Scottish Highlanders hung bundles of pearlwort over their doorways. Women placed the tiny weed under their right knee while giving birth to ensure fairies would not meddle with their newborn children.

Xochiquetzal lived on a mountain top surrounded by dancers and musicians. She was the Aztec godess of love--- and flowers. She was reknowned for her beauty and gaiety despite the fact that she was stolen from her true husband Taloc, the pulp of the earth, god of the mountains, rains and springs. Her male twin, Xochipilli, the prince of flowers, was the god of beauty, happiness, youth, music, dancing, and gamboling.

China: The mythical and august personage of jade, Queen Mother Wang Mu-Niang-Niang, wife of the Lord of the East, dwelled in the K'un-lun mountains, the abode of the immortals. There she presided over banquets, offering the other immortal gods feasts made primarily of P'an-t'ao, peaches of immortality, which ripened only once every three-thousand years in the imperial orchard. The peach presently symbolizes longevity in China.

Exotic marine Botanic Specimen From the
collection of Sylvia A. Earle.

Biology and Science

Behind the delicate fragrance and frail beauty of a flower is the tenacious life force of all plants. Capable of forging life from air, light, and soil, plants have colonized the entire surface of the earth while creating and maintaining the planet's atmosphere.

The secret to their success is their limitless capacity for change. Adaptation has produced plants in all forms, from the smallest microbodies to the tallest trees, with lifespans that measure from minutes to milleniums.

Small, squat, and primitive, the first terrestrial plant life appeared at the fringes of the sea 400 million years ago. Eons of evolution produced the angiosperms (flowering seed plants) and the less numerous gymnosperms (non-flowering seed plants) about 400 million years ago.

Natural selection and organic feats of bioengineering transformed aquatic algae into the diversity of plant species that live on land. To impede dehydration, landlocked plants acquired a semi-permeable outer membrane that lets moisture in and keeps it there. Where plants in watery surroundings had absorbed nutrients through their entire surface, their terrestrial cousins developed a vascular system to distribute food internally. Deprived of the sea's support, the new plants gained a structure that allowed them to defy gravity and reach for the sun. And, no longer travelers on the currents of the ocean, plants enlisted the aid of wind, insects, and animals to carry fertilizing pollen to other members of their species.

Exotic marine botanic specimen
From the collection of Sylvia A. Earle.

Green Kingdoms

WHAT'S IN A PLANT? SOME PLANT-LIKE LIVING THINGS, SUCH AS MUSHROOMS AND SEAWEED, ARE NOT ACTUALLY PLANTS, ALTHOUGH THEY SHARE CERTAIN CHARACTERISTICS. IN GENERAL, THE DISTINCTIONS BETWEEN PLANT-LIKE ORGANISMS AND TRUE PLANTS CENTER AROUND TWO DELICIOUS PREOCCUPATIONS: FOOD AND SEX.

THE KINGDOM PROTISTA INCLUDES PLANTS, SUCH AS ALGAE, DIATOMS, SLIME MOLDS, AND THAT DOMESTIC BANE, MILDEW, THAT THRIVE IN WATERY OR VERY MOIST HABITATS. MANY OF THESE SPECIES CAN MANUFACTURE THEIR OWN FOOD, BUT THEY LACK PLANT-LIKE STRUCTURES SUCH AS ROOTS AND LEAVES. THEY REPRODUCE EITHER BY RELEASING AN AQUATIC VERSION OF SPORES OR BY FRAGMENTATION, IN WHICH BROKEN-OFF BITS BECOME INDEPENDENT ORGANISMS.

THE KINGDOM FUNGI INCLUDES SMUTS, RUSTS, MUSHROOMS, TRUFFLES, YEAST, LICHENS, AND PENICILLIN, TO NAME A FEW SPECIES. INSTEAD OF PRODUCING THEIR OWN FOOD, FUNGI SERVE AS THE EARTH'S HOUSEKEEPERS AND RECYCLERS. AS THEY FEED UPON DEAD PLANTS AND ANIMALS, THE BREAKDOWN RELEASES NITROGEN, CARBON, AND OTHER ELEMENTS AND CREATES SOIL. MOST FUNGI ENGAGE IN SEXUAL REPRODUCTION, EXCHANGING MALE AND FEMALE SEX CELLS (CALLED GAMETES) BY MEANS OF SPORES.

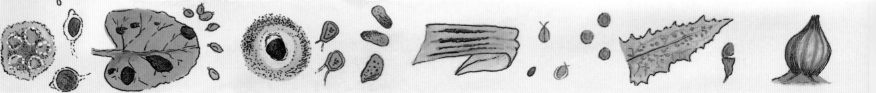

Of the more than 300,000 species of true plants in the kingdom Plantae, 250,000 are flowering angiosperms and 50,000 are non-flowering gymnosperms. The mostly green members of Plantae typically make their own food via photosynthesis, live in or on a substrate (such as soil), and are not mobile.

Older non-flowering families in the plant kingdom, such as club mosses, ferns, and horsetails, do not make seeds. They release spores consisting of a single cell that contains the genetic blueprint for a new plant. Because spores can germinate only if they land where conditions are just right, these plants produce millions of spores to increase their slim odds of survival.

Some plants reproduce without a partner by means of asexual processes. These methods come under the less-than-titillating heading of vegetative reproduction. Potato, bamboo and ginger plants extend rhizomes, underground horizontal stems that can take root and produce new plants. Strawberries and ground ivy send out creeping stems above the soil, which burrow back into the earth to create daughter plants. Mexican hat plants sprout buds on the edges of their leaves; the buds drop to the ground and grow into the next generation.

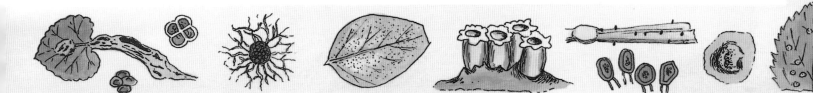

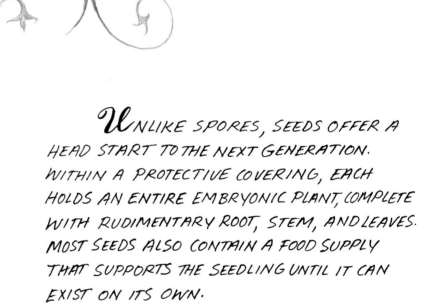

Kernels of life

Unlike spores, seeds offer a head start to the next generation. Within a protective covering, each holds an entire embryonic plant, complete with rudimentary root, stem, and leaves. Most seeds also contain a food supply that supports the seedling until it can exist on its own.

THE GYMNOSPERM CLASS OF SO-CALLED "NAKED SEED" PLANTS CONSISTS OF TWO GROUPS OF NON-FLOWERING, SEED-PRODUCING PLANTS. THE ANCIENT CYCADS ARE SIMILAR TO PALMS, WHILE THE CONIFEROUS EVERGREEN PINES ARE FAMILIAR AS CHRISTMAS TREES.

THE CONES OF CONIFER GYMNOSPERMS ARE THEIR REPRODUCTIVE STRUCTURES. LARGER THAN MALE CONES, FEMALE CONES DEVELOP HIGHER ON THE TREE. WIND-BORNE GRAINS OF POLLEN RELEASED BY MALE CONES MAKE THEIR WAY TO FEMALE CONES, WHERE THEY STICK TO A FLUID SURROUNDING THE OPENING OF THE OVULE. ACTUAL FERTILIZATION OCCURS MONTHS LATER.

WHEN THEY ARE READY TO GO TO SEED, SOME PLANTS LET IT FLY. TO TAKE ADVANTAGE OF THE WIND, THEY DISPERSE THEIR SEEDS VIA AIR MAIL. MAPLES HAVE WINGED NUTS, DANDELIONS HAVE TUFTS, AND OTHER SPECIES HAVE STREAMERS.

SOME PLANTS WITH HEAVY SEEDS GO BALLISTIC WHEN THE TIME IS RIPE. THE SEED PODS OF SPECIES SUCH AS GORSE, CRANESBILL, VIOLET AND BALSAM EXPLODE NOISILY, SHOOTING SEEDS OVER A WIDE AREA.

THE HITCHHIKING SEEDS OF AVERS AND AGRIMONY USE THEIR HOOKS TO CATCH A RIDE ON THE FUR OF WANDERING ANIMALS AND THE SWEATERS OF PASSING HIKERS.

AN OAK TREE CAN LIVE FOR ABOUT TWO HUNDRED YEARS. IN A GOOD YEAR, IT WILL PRODUCE 90,000 ACORNS. TWO HUNDRED TIMES 90,000 EQUALS....

"EVERY PART OF THIS EARTH
IS SACRED TO MY PEOPLE.
EVERY SHINING PINE NEEDLE--
WILL YOU TEACH YOUR CHILDREN
WHAT WE HAVE TAUGHT OUR
CHILDREN, THAT THE EARTH IS
OUR MOTHER? WHAT BEFALLS
THE EARTH BEFALLS THE SONS OF
THE EARTH. THIS WE KNOW.
THE EARTH DOES NOT BELONG
TO MAN. MAN BELONGS TO
THE EARTH"

-CHIEF SEATTLE, 1855

THE END OF THE LINE

EXTINCTION HAS BEEN A FACT OF LIFE EVER SINCE BLUE-GREEN ALGAE FIRST EMERGED FROM THE PRIMORDIAL OOZE. THE SPECIES OF PLANTS THAT EXIST TODAY ARE THE MODERN-DAY SURVIVORS OF THE ESTIMATED ONE BILLION PLANT AND ANIMAL SPECIES THAT NO LONGER EXIST.

ALL THE MAJOR EXTINCTIONS OF THE PAST OCCURED NATURALLY. CLIMATIC CHANGES LIKE THE ICE AGE, DISEASE, THE MYSTERIOUS NEMESIS OF THE DINOSAURS, AND OTHER SUCH PROCESSES WIPED OUT ANCIENT LIFE FORMS.

TODAY, HOWEVER, HUMANKIND'S MASSIVE IMPACT ON THE BIOSPHERE ACCOUNTS FOR ALMOST ALL PLANT AND ANIMAL EXTINCTIONS. THE RAPID GROWTH OF POPULATION AND INDUSTRY HAS OVERWHELMED THE EARTH'S NATURAL RECUPERATIVE POWERS, AND WE CANNOT COMPLETELY RELY ON TECHNOLOGICAL METHODS FOR UNDOING THE DAMAGE WE HAVE DONE.

BIOLOGISTS ESTIMATE THAT AS MANY AS 25,000 TO 30,000 SPECIES OF PLANTS ARE THREATENED, AND AS MANY AS 60,000 — A QUARTER OF THE TOTAL NUMBER OF KNOWN PLANTS -- COULD BECOME EXTINCT BY THE YEAR 2050. THIS RATE OF EXTINCTION IS AT LEAST 1,000 AND POSSIBLY 10,000 TIMES GREATER THAN THE RATE BEFORE THE INDUSTRIAL REVOLUTION.

KEY TO PRESERVING THE BLUE PLANET, THE DIVERSITY OF LIVING THINGS WITHIN A SPECIES OR AN ECOSYSTEM HAS ENABLED LIFE TO REBOUND FROM THE EDGE OF CATASTROPHY TIME AND AGAIN. EACH SPECIES OCCUPIES A UNIQUE NICHE IN THE FOOD WEB, CONNECTED TO THE WHOLE BY ONLY A SMALL NUMBER OF OTHER SPECIES. ELIMINATE ONE SPECIES, AND A HOLE IS TORN IN THE INTRICATE FABRIC THAT TOOK MILLIONS OF YEARS TO WEAVE. HOW MANY HOLES WILL IT TAKE BEFORE THE ENTIRE SYSTEM UNRAVELS?

You're gonna reap what you sow

SUTTONS SEEDS LTD. TORQUAY

MOTHER EARTH KNOWS THAT DIVERSITY, CO-OPERATION, AND PARTNERSHIP SUSTAIN LIFE. INSPIRED BY HER WISDOM, A NEW BREED OF "PLANT PEOPLE" IS TRANSFORMING VISIONARY GARDEN-CENTRIC IDEAS INTO SEEDS OF CHANGE.

LIKE GREEN GOLD IN THE SAVINGS BANK OF EVOLUTION, SEEDS ARE LIVING TREASURES. EACH CONTAINS A DROP FROM THE EARTH'S GENE POOL, WHICH IS FILLED WITH EONS OF ADAPTATION.

GONE TO SEED: PIONEERS OF PRESERVATION, MODERN-DAY BIO-EXPLORERS COLLECT, TRADE, GROW, AND STORE DIVERSE SEEDS IN SEED BANKS. THESE SEEDS YIELD A HARVEST NOT ONLY OF SUCCULENT PRODUCE BUT OF HARDIER, PEST-RESISTANT STRAINS AND MORE SEEDS. IN AN ENDLESS CYCLE OF REGENERATION, EACH GENERATION OF SEEDS PRODUCES IMPROVED OFFSPRING.

Seeds of Change
ORGANICALLY GROWN SEEDS
BRANDYWINE TOMATO

SHEPHERD'S GARDEN SEEDS
WATERMELON
MOON AND STARS
American Heirloom
Contents 15–20 seeds

Personal growth: far from the farm, in the urban jungle, a grassroots movement has taken hold. Where broken glass and crumpled metal once glittered in vacant lots, carefully tended gardens and plants now shimmer like emeralds. People cut off from the economic and social mainstream cultivate self-esteem and new skills on these plots, learning nature's most optimistic lessons. Dirt, water, seeds, and sunshine turn into food to eat and to sell. Urban farmers can find a new job and a new life on these green streets.

Garbancito

French Horticultural

Vermont Appaloosa

Wren's Egg

Phipps Ranch Pebble Bean

Fava Bean

Turtle Bean

Brown Speckled Cow

Jacob's Cattle Bean

Snowcap Bean

Rio Zape Bean

Madeira

Bayo Bean

Christmas Lima

Flor de Junio

New Mexico Appalousa

Red Appaloosa

Buckskin

Raquel

Spanish Tolosanas

Ojo De Cabra
(Eye of The Goat)

Jumbo Pinto Runner

Tongues of Fire

Jackson
Wonder Lima

Scarlet Runner

Anasazi

Rattlesnake Bean

Black
Valentine

Florida Speckled Butter Bean

Borlotti

Bolita

Steuben Yellow-eye

Hand Trowel

Iron Turf Lifter

Grass Shear

Fisherman's Weeder

English Garden Broom

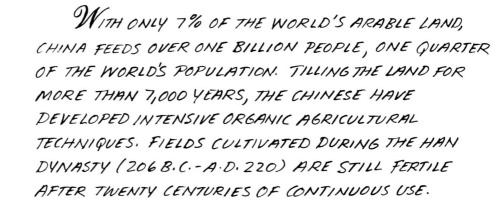

"LEAVE THIS TREE ALONE... IT IS JUST LIKE GOD. TO WORSHIP IT IS TO LET THE FIELDS GROW BETTER."
CHINESE PROVERB

WITH ONLY 7% OF THE WORLD'S ARABLE LAND, CHINA FEEDS OVER ONE BILLION PEOPLE, ONE QUARTER OF THE WORLD'S POPULATION. TILLING THE LAND FOR MORE THAN 7,000 YEARS, THE CHINESE HAVE DEVELOPED INTENSIVE ORGANIC AGRICULTURAL TECHNIQUES. FIELDS CULTIVATED DURING THE HAN DYNASTY (206 B.C.–A.D. 220) ARE STILL FERTILE AFTER TWENTY CENTURIES OF CONTINUOUS USE.

IN THE CHAGRA, THEIR "GARDEN-IN-THE-FOREST," THE INDIGENOUS PEOPLE OF COLOMBIA GROW CROPS SUCH AS YUCCA, AVOCADO, PAPAYA, MANGO, LEMON AND PEPPERS. MIMICKING NATURE, THEY REMOVE AS FEW TREES AS POSSIBLE TO CREATE FOREST CLEARINGS THAT ADMIT JUST ENOUGH LIGHT FOR CROP GROWTH. THEY CULTIVATE A CHAGRA FOR NO MORE THAN A FEW YEARS AND THEN MOVE ON TO ALLOW THE JUNGLE TO RECLAIM AND REJUVENATE THE LAND. EACH GROUP'S HEADMAN GUIDES HIS PEOPLE SO AS TO SATISFY THEIR NEED FOR FOOD, FIBER, AND FUEL WHILE LEAVING A MAXIMUM OF THEIR ENVIRONMENT SACRED TO NATURE.

Glass Cloche   *Hand Weeder*

Long-Reach Pruner

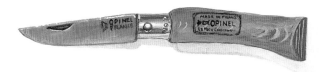

GOOD FARMERS ARE ARTISTS. THEY PAINT THE
LANDSCAPE WITH SQUASH, CORN, CELERY, BEANS,
AND A CORNUCOPIA OF OTHER FRUITS AND
VEGETABLES. THEIR TOOLS ARE THE RAKE, THE HOE,
THE PITCHFORK, THE SHOVEL, AND THE SHEARS.
LIKE ALL ARTISTS, THEY SEEK TO BALANCE
TECHNIQUE WITH HEART AND HARMONY.

IN THE ANDES, ON THE VELDT,
IN PROVENCE, OR ON THE MESA, VITAL
KNOWLEDGE IS PASSED DOWN IN
SEEDS THAT CONTAIN WHOLE
CULTURAL HISTORIES. A
SEED HOLDS THE TALE OF A
SOCIETY'S ADAPTION TO ITS
ENVIRONMENT AND ITS
SOLUTION TO THE PROBLEMS
OF NUTRITION AND TASTE.

AGRICULTURE
IS
CULTURE

BEANS

VOLUNTEER

GARDENING
HORTICULTURE
U.S. POSTAGE 3

Hand Fork

New World Foods

"Sometimes I come to the field in the evening and stay all night because the porcupines were eating my corn. I'd sing all the way up and down the rows. My Dad said his corn is like children and you have to sing to them and they will be happy." —CITIZEN OF HOPILAND, ARIZONA

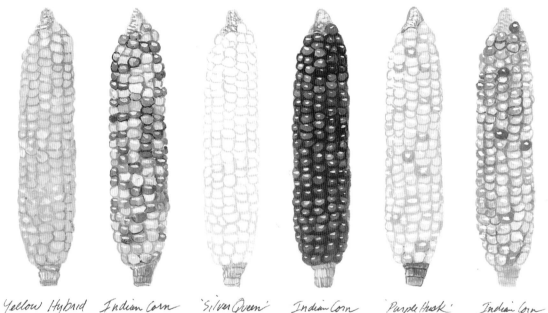

Yellow Hybrid   Indian Corn   'Silver Queen'   Indian Corn   'Purple Husk'   Indian Corn

THE SPANISH CONQUISTADORES CAME TO THE NEW WORLD IN SEARCH OF GREAT RICHES. AS THEY PLUNDERED THE GOLD-RICH EMPIRES OF MEXICO AND PERU, THEY CAME UPON VEGETABLE TREASURES AS WELL. IN THIS ENDEAVOR THEY WERE JOINED BY ENGLISH, FRENCH, PORTUGUESE, AND DUTCH EXPLORERS. CORN KERNELS LIKE PEARLS, TOMATOES RED AS RUBIES, EMERALD-GREEN BELL PEPPERS, AND OTHER LIVING GEMS CHANGED FOREVER THE CUISINE AND DIET OF EUROPE.

THE CLASSIC ITALIAN AUTUMN MEAL — POLENTA (CORN MEAL MUSH) WITH TOMATO SAUCE, ROASTED PEPPERONCINI (TUSCAN PEPPERS), AND PATATE AL FORNO (OVEN-ROASTED POTATOES) — IS A CULTURAL COLLAGE OF FOODS FROM NOBLE NORTH AND SOUTH AMERICAN EMPIRES.

Early Girl —   Italian Costoluto   Purple Calabash —   Green Bell Pepper   Elberta Girl —

*I*N THE HIGH DESERT OF THE AMERICAN SOUTHWEST, THE ANNUAL CORN CROP IS A TESTIMONY TO THE SKILL AND SPIRITUAL TENACITY OF THE PUEBLO INDIANS. FOR CENTURIES, THE HOPI, ZUNI, AND OTHER PUEBLO PEOPLES HAVE COAXED FOOD FROM THE SANDY SOIL AND CALLED ON THE RAIN TO WATER THEIR FIELDS.

*E*UROPEANS FIRST SOUGHT THE TOMATO AS AN APHRODISIAC. BEFORE LONG, HOWEVER, THE PURITANS OF NEW ENGLAND DECLARED THE 'LOVE-APPLES' POISONOUS. PERHAPS THE STRAIGHT-LACED SETTLERS DISAPPROVED OF THE OBVIOUS SENSUAL PLEASURE THAT NATIVE AMERICANS, WHOM THEY CONSIDERED AGENTS OF SATAN, FOUND IN THE TOMATO PATCH.

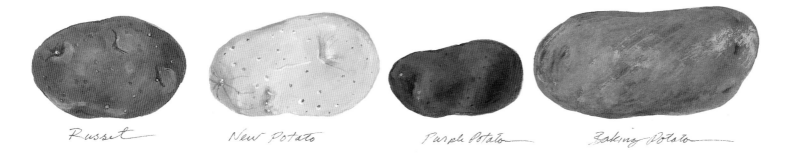

Russet —   New Potato   Purple Potato —   Baking Potato —

*T*RACE THE ORIGINS OF THE HUMBLE POTATO ON YOUR PLATE AND A TALE OF UPHEAVAL, ADVENTURE, MIGRATION, FAMINE, AND WAR UNFOLDS. THE INCAS EXPERIMENTED WITH THOUSANDS OF VARIETIES OF POTATOES TO ENSURE THEIR SURVIVAL SHOULD ONE SPECIES FAIL. OTHER NATIVE AMERICANS ALSO DISCOVERED THE TUBER'S VERSATILITY AND ABILITY TO SUSTAIN, BUT EUROPE'S FIRST POTATO EATERS WERE EPICURES WHO SAVORED THE DELICACY FOR ITS SUPPOSED POWER TO CURE IMPOTENCE. EVENTUALLY, THE POTATO MADE ITS WAY TO THE POOREST OF EUROPEAN TABLES. IRISH POTATO FARMERS COULD HAVE LEARNED FROM THE INCAS, FOR A SINGLE VARIETY DOMINATED IRELAND'S DIET. MILLIONS STARVED WHEN DISEASE DESTROYED THEIR CROP.

Wild Rice

Arborio Rice

Brown Basmati Rice

Valencia Rice

American Brown Basmati Rice

Sambal Short-grain Rice

Jasmine Sticky Rice

Red Rice

Wild Pecan Rice

Sri Lankan Red Rice

Short-Grained Brown Rice

THE STAFF OF LIFE

To BE CERTAIN, IN THE EVOLUTIONARY SENSE YOU ARE WHAT YOU EAT.

SURPRISINGLY, AS FEW AS FIFTEEN STAPLE CROPS STAND BETWEEN HUMANKIND AND STARVATION. WHEAT AND RICE COMPRISE THREE QUARTERS OF THE WORLD'S CEREAL GRAIN PRODUCTION, PROVIDING HALF OF ALL HUMAN PROTEIN REQUIREMENTS. FIVE OTHER GRASSES -- MILLET, BARLEY, OATS, RYE, CORN, AND SORGHUM--PRODUCE THE FOURTH QUARTER OF THE PLANET'S GRAIN OUTPUT. THE REMAINDER OF THE WORLD'S AGRICULTURAL OUTPUT FOR THE MOST PART CONSISTS OF VARIOUS KINDS OF LEGUMES (ESPECIALLY LENTILS, PEAS, AND BEANS), ROOT CROPS (MOSTLY CASSAVA, SWEET POTATOES, AND YAMS), AND MISCELLANEA (BANANAS, COCONUTS, AND SUGAR CANE, AMONG OTHERS).

"Wisdom, power, and goodness meet in the bounteous field of wheat."
THE WHEATFIELD, HANNAH FLAGG GOULD, 1789-1865

Millet

Rice

Oats

Black Japonica Rice

Carnaroli Rice

Converted Rice

Gobind Bhog Rice

Wheani Rice

Long-Grained Brown Rice

Black Sticky Rice

Sticky Brown Rice

Short-Grained Red Rice

Manzanella Rice

THE POTENTIAL OF SOYA FROM THE SOYBEAN PLANT HAS YET TO BE REALIZED IN THE WEST. FOR CENTURIES A STAPLE FOOD IN ASIA, SOYA CAN BE PROCESSED INTO OIL, TOFU, SOY SAUCE, SOY MILK, AND MORE. HIGH IN PROTEIN, LOW ON THE FOOD CHAIN, AND LOW IN CHOLESTEROL, IT IS THE PERFECT FOOD FOR THE 21ST CENTURY.

LET THEM EAT CAKE : MARIE ANTOINETTE SHOULD HAVE KNOWN THAT HER SUGGESTION WOULD HERALD HER DEMISE, FOR IN FRANCE, AS IN MANY PLACES, THE DAILY BREAD IS THE STAFF OF LIFE. THE FRENCH IDIOM "TO TAKE THE BREAD OUT OF SOMEONE'S MOUTH" MEANS TO DEPRIVE THEM OF THEIR LIVELIHOOD.

SUPERSTITION AND TABOO UNDERSCORE BREAD'S IMPORTANCE. A CROSS MARKED ON BREAD DOUGH BEFORE BAKING WOULD PREVENT THE LOAF FROM FALLING INTO THE HANDS OF SATAN. BREAD BAKED ON GOOD FRIDAY WAS SAID TO RETAIN ITS FRESHNESS LONGER, AND THE WOMAN WHO BAKED IT WAS SAID TO BE BLESSED. THE RUSSIANS, HOWEVER, BELIEVED THAT BAKING BREAD ON ANY FRIDAY WAS BAD LUCK. IN WESTERN EUROPE, HOUSEHOLDS SAFEGUARDED THEIR HEALTH BY HANGING A LOAF OF BREAD MADE WITH GRAIN FROM THE FIRST HARVEST FROM THE CEILING. STALE BREAD WAS PLACED IN CRADLES IN BELGIUM TO PROTECT THE BABES WITHIN. IN MOROCCO, BREAD WAS USED AS A CURE FOR STAMMERING.

Rye

Sorghum

Barley

Soft Wheat

Grassland

Amber Waves

For 12,000 years or more, the indigenous people of the North American prairie hunted herds of bison that fed on buffalo grass and blue grama. As they voyaged across the vast golden sea between the Allegheny and Rocky Mountains, the nomadic buffalo transported seeds in their fur, broke the soil with their hooves and enriched it with their droppings.

Such virgin grasslands are now rare, long since supplanted by fields of European wheat or pastures of Kentucky bluegrass imported from Eurasian steppes. Prairie grasses are relegated to the status of weeds, but weeds are really just plants we haven't found a use for yet.

Efforts to crossbreed prairie grasses with hardy strains of other cereal grains may yield new sources of food for our hungry planet. Botanists hope to tap the extraordinary survival instincts of the weeds in order to produce edible grains that can withstand difficult growing conditions. Reaching deep into the soil with their roots, prairie grasses can find water and nutrients that lie far beyond the grasp of most cultivated root systems. Weedy tenacity can be witnessed in any city of the world, where green sprouts appear in every sidewalk crack.

The savannah is the tropical version of the prairie. Cleared and renewed by frequent natural fires, savannah vegetation includes trees. In Africa, grassland studded with acacia and thorny scrub feeds grazing species such as zebra, wildebeast, antelope, giraffe, elephant, and black rhino. Eucalyptus trees dot the Australian savannah, serving as the main food source of the koala bear; mobs of kangaroos bound about their daily lives on the open grassland. Referred to as llanos in Venezuela and Columbia and as campos and cerados in Brazil, the South American savannah is home to drought and fire-resistant trees.

 Black Peppercorns

 Cardamom

 Nutmeg

 Cloves

 Lombok Chilies

Garlic

White Mustard Seed

Negro Chilean

Caraway

Clove Buds

The Spice of Life

In the middle ages, nearly twenty different spices were traded between Europe and the East. Among them, pepper acquired the greatest trade value and represented almost half the spice imports in Venice for close to a century. The near-monopoly of Venetians in the spice trade made their enchanted city one of the richest of the time.

Before refrigeration, Europeans preserved their meat with salt, and it was made palatable again only with the addition of pepper. A bulwark against famine when crops failed, salted meat also made long sea voyages possible. In the early 1980's, the recovery of a 1545 shipwreck, the British Royal Navy ship Mary Rose, illustrated the traditional value of pepper. Almost all the skeletal sailors found inside had little bags in their pockets filled not with coins of silver and gold but with peppercorns.

 Cinnamon Sticks

 Sesame Seed

Green Peppercorns

Saffron Threads

 Juniper Berries

Allspice

Crushed Red Pepper

Fennel Seed

Star Anise

Pickling Spice

Ginger

Black Sesame Seed

Pink Peppercorns

Dried Turmeric

Cumin Seeds

Guajillo Chilis

In EVERY CULTURE, FOOD IS A SYMBOL THAT COMMEMORATES AND CELEBRATES SPIRITUAL BELIEFS. THE ANCIENT EGYPTIANS SWORE OATHS ON THE ONION, WHICH REPRESENTED THE MANY-LAYERED UNIVERSE. ROMAN CATHOLICS AND ANGLICANS TAKE COMMUNION IN THE FORM OF WINE AND WAFERS. RICE IS THE SOURCE OF SPIRITUAL INSPIRATION FOR THE MALAYS.

Black Pepper

Poppy Seeds

Vanilla Bean

White Peppercorns

DIVINE BEVERAGES: TWO BEANS & A LEA

The ancients considered chocolate, coffee, and tea gifts from the gods. For milleniums, the precious trio has been prepared in decoctions, brewed in beverages, and combined with food. Their sublime flavors and stimulating effects have inspired fantasy, rapture, rebellion, cults, and craving.

Traditional coffee stories describe its exhilerating effects on the body. Long enjoyed by Ethiopian travelers and warriors, coffee berries were mashed into a paste, mixed with suet, formed into balls, and eaten. The stimulant was supposedly discovered by a goatherd named Kaldi, who observed his flock prancing about at sunrise after eating some red berries. Kaldi sampled the fruit from the surrounding bushes and soon joined the goats in their antics.

Coffee

ORIGINALLY FROM CHINA, TEA IS SAID TO HAVE BEEN DISCOVERED BY SHEN NUNG, THE DIVINE CULTIVATOR. WHILE PRUNING HIS CELESTIAL CAMELLIA BUSHES, HE SAW A LEAF FALL INTO A NEARBY POT OF BOILING WATER. UPON SAMPLING THE UNEXPECTED LIQUOR, SHEN NUNG DECLARED IT SIMPLY DIVINE AND GAVE IT TO HUMANKIND AS A GIFT.

QUETZALCOATL, THE WHITE-BEARED AZTEC GOD OF WISDOM AND KNOWLEDGE, INTRODUCED XOCOATL (CHOCOLATE) TO THE AZTEC COURT. HE SERVED IT TO SOLDIERS AND RULERS, THE ONLY PEOPLE HE TRUSTED WITH ITS POWERS. INDEED, THE BOTANICAL NAME FOR THE COCOA TREE IS THEOBROMA COCOA, WHICH TRANSLATES AS "FOOD OF THE GODS." FEW WOULD DISAGREE WITH THAT ASSESSMENT OF THE SCRUMPTIOUS BEAN.

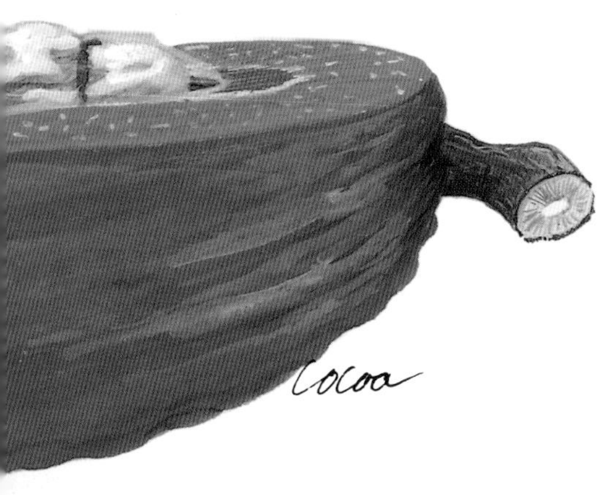

Cocoa

Tea

Parkinson: "Paradisus", Title Page, 1629

Contemplating Global Gardens

Gardens, where nature and civilization meet, reflect our eternal struggle to tame the earth and at the same time savor its beauty. Timeless and tranquil, gardens shelter us both from the hubbub of human activity and the rigors of the wilderness.

The religions of the world have employed the garden as a symbol for peace and paradise as well as for sin and temptation. In the earthly realm, gardens such as Louis XIV's Versailles and the White House Rose Garden have served as emblems of political power. As a medium for artistic expression, the garden has been the canvas upon which hobbyists and landscape architects create wonders of beauty.

An intermediary between the indoors and out, the garden links us with our world. From house plants and window boxes to orchards and meadows, gardens are private and ordered yet wild at heart. Urban parks and botanical gardens provide a respite from everyday stresses and a stage for new and different experiences. As celebrations of life, town and country gardens alike join humankind's finest impulses with nature's most elemental.

Kumquat

THE
GARDENS
OF
Islam
AND
India

A DESERT NOMAD DREAMS OF COOL SHADE, RUNNING BROOKS, FLOWERS, FRUIT, AND PERFUMED BREEZES. BORN IN THE DESERTS OF THE ARABIAN PENINSULA, ISLAM EMBRACED GREEN GARDENS AS A KIND OF HEAVEN ON EARTH, A FORETASTE OF THE SENSUAL PARADISE TO COME. WITHIN PROTECTIVE GARDEN WALLS, THE DEVOTED COULD TAKE REFUGE FROM THE TUMULT OF THE WORLD AND CONTEMPLATE THE TRANQUILITY OF THE VIRTUOUS SOUL.

DIVIDED INTO FOUR QUARTERS BY CANALS THAT MET AT A CENTRAL CIRCULAR BASIN, ISLAMIC GARDENS FOUND THEIR SIGNIFICANCE IN SYMMETRY. ISLAMIC NOTIONS ABOUT FORM AND MEANING COMBINED BABYLONIAN AND HINDU THINKING, AS WELL AS THE THEORIES OF THE GREEK PHILOSOPHER PYTHAGORAS. IN THE GARDEN, SQUARE SHAPES REPRESENTED NATURE'S MULTIPLE MANIFESTATIONS AND THE CIRCLE EVOKED THE RECURRING CYCLE OF LIFE. AN OPEN-AIR VERSION OF ISLAMIC ARCHITECTURE, GARDEN DESIGN HAS THROUGH THE CENTURIES REMAINED A WAY TO EXPRESS A SPIRITUAL UNDERSTANDING OF THE UNIVERSE.

MUSLIMS CONSIDERED THE KNOWLEDGE OF PLANTS AND THEIR PRACTICAL USES A PART OF DIVINE CREATION TO BE SHARED BY ALL. HORTICULTURALISTS AND PHYSICIANS RECORDED THE CHARACTERISTICS OF ROSES, LAVENDER, RUE, CORIANDER, CUMIN, MINT, OPIUM POPPIES, THYME, ASPARAGUS, CHERRIES, FIGS, JUJUBES, APPLES, APRICOTS, MULBERRIES, ORANGES, PLUMS, AND OTHER PLANTS.

ISLAMIC GARDEN ART REACHED ITS PEAK IN THE MOGUL GARDENS OF INDIA. KNOWN AS "THE FIRST GARDENER," BABUR (ZAHIR UD-DIN MUHAMMAD) CONQUERED INDIA AND FOUNDED THE MOGUL EMPIRE IN THE 1520s. OVER THE NEXT TWO CENTURIES, HE AND HIS SUCCESSORS LAID OUT AND BUILT SOME OF THE MOST BEAUTIFUL GARDENS EVER SEEN. THEY BECAME PART OF THE PLAIN AND LAKELAND PANORAMA OF NORTHERN INDIA, ALONGSIDE THE WILDFLOWER MEADOWS, POPLAR-LINED AVENUES, AND PINE-COVERED MOUNTAINS.

Japanese Gardens

"NOT YET HAVING BECOME A BUDDHA,
THIS ANCIENT PINE TREE,
IDLY DREAMING."

— ISSA

The Japanese believed that kami, divine spirits, could manifest themselves in mountains, trees, stones, and other things. They sought contact with the kami in nature, and to that end created gardens that would attract the deities and foster spiritual contemplation.

A pure and graceful form emerged: the rock garden. Stones personified the kami and evoked the passage of time; sand and gravel represented life's fluid yet enduring aspect; and water played its part as the island country's most prominent natural feature.

The first Japanese gardens included no vegetation. But as the garden evolved into an idealized version of the natural landscape, trees and grasses were added to suggest the windswept shoreline. Pine trees were particularly suited to Japanese gardening, for their branches are easily trained.

HOPING TO CREATE AN UNCLUTTERED EFFECT, GARDENERS REFINED ELABORATE PRUNING TECHNIQUES THAT ARE STILL USED TODAY. THEY CAREFULLY PLUCKED INDIVIDUAL PINE NEEDLES AND TRIMMED BRANCHES TO PERFECT THE FORM OF EACH TREE. TAKEN TO THE EXTREME, THESE METHODS SPAWNED THE ART OF BONSAI, IN WHICH SEEDLING TREES ARE PLACED IN EARTHENWARE POTS AND TWISTED, WRAPPED, AND CLIPPED ALMOST DAILY TO STUNT THEIR GROWTH. WHEN SPACE FOR FULL-SCALE GARDENING GREW SCARCE IN CROWDED JAPAN, THE ART OF BONSAI BECAME INCREASINGLY POPULAR.

THOUGH FLOWERS ARE AN ACCENT, NOT THE FOCUS, IN THE JAPANESE GARDEN, THE JAPANESE CELEBRATE WITH A CULT-LIKE REVERENCE CHERRY BLOSSOMS, AZALEAS, CHRYSANTHEMUMS, AND IRISES AT THE PEAK OF THEIR LIFE-CYCLES.

*F*ORMAL GARDENING CAME TO ENGLAND FROM FRANCE IN THE 18TH CENTURY. BEFORE LONG, ENGLISH GARDENERS ITCHED FOR MORE FREEDOM. BOTANIST JOSEPH ADDISON EXPRESSED THIS RESTLESSNESS IN THE SPECTATOR OF JUNE 25, 1712: "OUR BRITISH GARDENERS, INSTEAD OF HUMORING NATURE, LOVE TO DEVIATE FROM IT AS MUCH AS POSSIBLE. OUR TREES RISE IN CONES, GLOBES AND PYRAMIDS. WE SEE THE MARKS OF SISSARS ON EVERY PLANT AND BUSH... I WOULD RATHER LOOK UPON A TREE IN ALL ITS LUXURIANCY AND DIFFUSION OF BOUGHS AND BRANCHES, THAN WHEN IT IS THUS CUT AND TRIMMED INTO A MATHEMATICAL FIGURE."

Eccentric English Gardens

The English became horticultural pioneers, collecting plants, disseminating botanical knowledge, breeding a rhapsody of new blooms, and returning formal parks to their "natural" state as fields and wildflower meadows.

Scrambling to keep up with the blossoming movement toward "natural" gardening, one eminent English town gardener put the following out-of-date topiary up for sale:

"St. George in his box; his arm scarce long enough, but will be in condition to stick in the dragon by next April.

The tower of Babel, not yet finished.

A pair of giants stunted to be sold cheap.

A quickset hog, shot up into porcupine, by being forgot a week in rainy weather.

A Queen Elizabeth in phlyrea a little inclining to the green sickness, but full of growth."

The apparent spontaneity of the 18th century English cottage garden in fact reflected careful planning. Gardeners drew up groundplans, elevations, and cross-sections that took into account a plot's exposure, soil conditions, and function. And, of course, the designers always kept beauty in mind.

Topiary

For centuries, garden artists have hewn thickly leaved evergreen shrubs—such as the cypress, box, rosemary, box honeysuckle, holly, and yew—into living sculptures. Few early examples of the ephemeral art of topiary survive today.

Topiary was invented in the 1st century by a friend of Roman Emperor Augustus, a proponent of agriculture and the arts. Originally a method of training shrubs into border hedges, topiary became a means of accenting the garden scene with cones, spires, and columns.

$\mathcal{B}$Y THE 18TH CENTURY, THE ART OF THE TREE BARBER BROKE AWAY FROM CLASSICAL DESIGN TO INDULGE IN BAROQUE WHIMSY. SHORN SHIPS SAILED ACROSS LAWNS AND BUSHY FOXES WERE PERPETUALLY CHASED BY LEAFY HOUNDS.

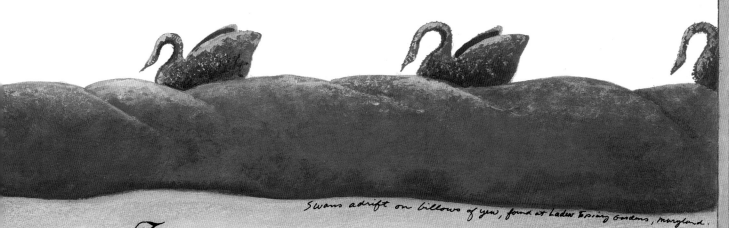

Swans adrift on billows of yew, found at Ladew Spring Gardens, Maryland.

$\mathcal{T}$OPIARY ACHIEVED ITS MOST FASHIONABLE EXPRESSION IN THE NETHERLANDS, FRANCE, AND ENGLAND. KNOWN AS TREE MASONS, ENGLISH LEAF SCULPTORS TOOK ADVANTAGE OF AN ABUNDANT SUPPLY OF SUITABLE INDIGENOUS PLANTS. PARTICULARLY IN ENGLAND, THEIR ART REMAINS A LIVELY ONE TODAY.

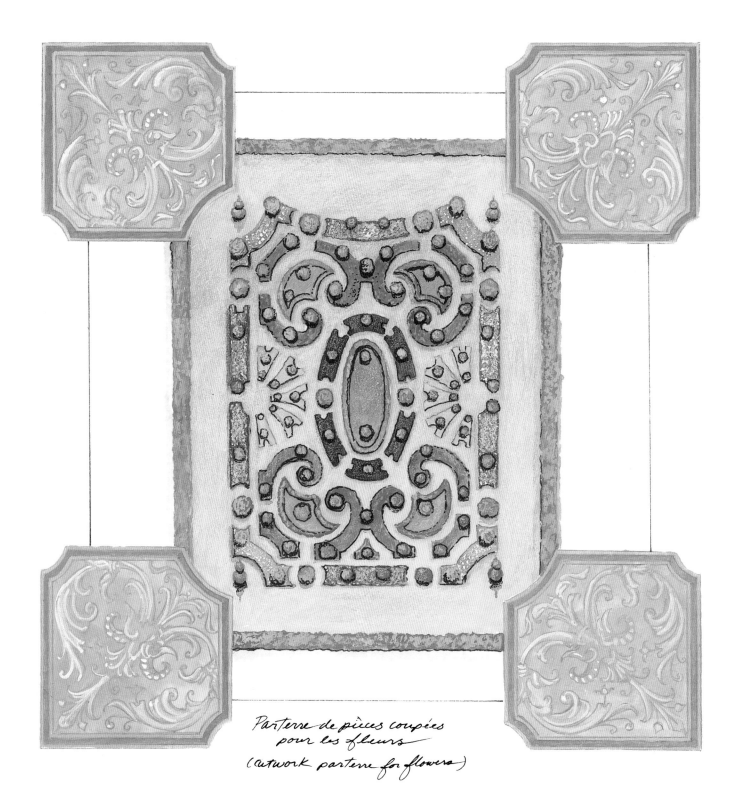

Parterre de pièces coupées
pour les fleurs

(cutwork parterre for flowers)

Formal French Gardens

Emerging from medieval feudalism to become a national monarchy, France sought to expand its borders. On campaigns into Italy, French armies admired that country's accomplishments in the fine arts and garden design. They returned to France with plans to recreate the drama of the controlled, stylized gardens they saw.

King of France from 1643 to 1715, Louis XIV built the monumental gardens at Versailles. With vistas of plants on parade stretching to the horizon and hedge sentries guarding intricately ornate flower beds, the gardens demonstrated the Sun King's power over nature. The fame of these gardens was so great that even the Emperor of China wanted to copy them. He devoted a small part of the extensive gardens at the summer palace in Peking to "foreign water works." Chinese observers called the western designs Hsieh Ch'i Ch'u (harmonious, strange, and pleasant).

Back in France, Louis XIV developed a staggering appetite for flowers. During the 1672 season alone, 10,000 tuberoses were grown in Avignon and transported to Versailles. Columbines, carnations, pinks, irises, lilies, and peonies were shipped in from all over Europe; helianthus arrived from the English colonies in North America; and tropical canna came from Mexico.

To keep the Sun King in flowers all winter, the royal gardener designed hothouses and conservatories. The royal practice soon made the cultivation of exotic and rare plants a favorite winter pastime for the French gentry.

A contemporary French pastime: drinking pastis in the garden. This sublime liqueur, flavored with aniseed is great for digesting a meal and the gossip of the day.

LA MAISON
ET LE JARDIN
DE RENOIR
AUX COLLETTES

104
CAGNES-S-MER

Musée Renoir
du Souvenir
CAGNES-SUR-MER

ENTRÉE : 20,00 F

Nᵒ J45239

RENOIR MCMXII

Renoir

'Landscape at les Collettes' Pierre Auguste Renoir 1910

GALERIE BEAUBOURG
CHATEAU NOTRE-DAME DES FLEURS
06140 VENCE

WINSOR & NEWTON
DESIGNERS
GOUACHE
OLIVE
GREEN
14 ml ℮
0.47 US fl.oz.

'A Sunday on la Grande Jatte' Topiary Park
OLD DEAF SCHOOL PARK
COLUMBUS, OHIO

THE FINE ART GARDEN

"MORE THAN ANYTHING I MUST
HAVE FLOWERS, ALWAYS, ALWAYS"
- CLAUDE MONET

"Water Lilies" Claude Monet 1906

Claude Monet 190

ACADÉMIE DES BEAUX ARTS

—

Jardin Claude Monet

—

ENTRÉE 15 F.

No 4649

LES FLEURS

FLOWER SEEDS

"A Sunday on la Grande Jatte"
Georges Seurat - 1884

PERM. LEMON YE

VAN GOGH

WATER COLOUR

JAUNE CITRON PERM.

VAN GOGH SUNFLOWER 35 SEEDS

#3770

Cabbage

Alpine Strawberry

Oak

Jasmine

Grape

Chrysanthemum

Violet

Cherry

Holly

Ivy

French Lace Geranium

Eucalyptus

Maple

Daphne

Strawberry

Elm

Oak

Scented Geranium

"If you can paint one leaf
you can paint the whole world."

RUSKIN

No blue leaves

Our world is tinted by a solar paintbrush. Many of the colors we see are made of reflected light – the leftovers, as it were, of the world's meal of absorbed wavelengths.

Chlorophyll molecules absorb mainly blue and red light, the wavelengths most effective in photosynthesis. The other colors are discarded by the busy plant, and are literally reflected from the surface of leaves as the color green.

"Leaves are the verbs that conjugate the seasons"

*T*OWARD THE END OF SUMMER, THE SHORTER DAYS REMIND TREES TO PREPARE FOR WINTER. TO FORTIFY THEIR TRUNKS AND ROOTS FOR THE HARSH SEASON AHEAD, TREES HOARD NUTRIENTS DEEP WITHIN. A CORKY LAYER OF CELLS FORMS AT THE BASE OF EACH LEAF'S STEM, CHOKING OFF ITS SUPPLY OF FOOD. AS THE LEAVES STARVE, PHOTOSYNTHESIS AND CHLOROPHYLL PRODUCTION CEASES. STRIPPED OF THEIR GREEN CAMOUFLAGE, LEAVES REVEAL THEIR TRUE COLORS, THE VIVID SCARLET SECRET KEPT THROUGHOUT THE SUMMER.

THE SOLACE OF OPEN SPACES   GRETEL EHRLICH, 1985

Barking up the Right Tree

Although a tree's layer of bark is dead tissue, it is essential to survival. Up to a foot thick, as on the giant redwoods and sequoias, or paper-thin, as on the birch, bark protects the delicate workings of a tree's sapwood and the living xylem and phloem within. Just peeling the chalky white strips from a birch tree can endanger its sapwood.

The cork oak of the Mediterranean region has such a thick bark of quality cork that cork harvesters can cut it off the tree in slabs several inches thick. Careful not to harm the tree, the harvesters can return in ten years to collect another batch of cork.

The dark, rich color of redwood bark is the product of a high concentration of tannin, a bitter chemical that repels insects and fungi.

Bark contains air holes, called lenticels, that allow the tree to breathe.

The native Americans of eastern North America made roofs, canoes, and shoes from the thin bark of the hardy, fast-growing birch, for it is impervious to water.

TREE HOUSES: A ROOM WITH A VIEW

"TO CLIMB UP, UP AMONG THE LEAVES, BEYOND THE REACH OF INTERVENTION, MUST BE THE OLDEST, MOST JOYOUS INSTINCT IN THE WORLD, THE NEXT BEST THING TO FLYING."

GREEN THOUGHTS, ELEANOR PERÉNYI, 1981

AFFICIONADOS OF AUTUMN FOLIAGE, THE JAPANESE BUILT PATHS ON STILTS AMONG THE TREES SO THEY COULD VIEW THE MYRIAD OF BRILLIANT ORANGES AND REDS UP CLOSE.

THE ITALIANS CREATED GREEN ROOMS WITH THEIR TREES: BY CAREFULLY PRUNING AND INTERWEAVING BRANCHES, THEY WOULD CRAFT WITHIN THE BOUGHS A SPHERE OF SPACE WHERE ONE COULD PLACE A CHAIR AND SIT PEACEFULLY.

GUARDIANS OF THE FOOD CHAIN, TIMBER TREES ARE THE LIFE FORCE OF THE FORESTS. IN A SINGLE TREE, INSECTS FIND SHELTER UNDER THE BARK AND FOOD IN THE LEAVES, BIRDS EAT THE INSECTS, SQUIRRELS FEAST ON NUTS OR BERRIES, OWLS NEST IN THE BRANCHES AND TRUNK, AND SMALL ANIMALS MAKE HOMES IN BURROWS UNDER THE ROOTS. LIKEWISE, IVY CLIMBS THE BRANCHES TOWARD SUNLIGHT, VAMPIRIC MISTLETOE SUCKS SAP FROM THE OAK'S HIGH LIMBS, FERNS AND FLOWERS GROW FROM DEBRIS IN BRANCH JOINTS, AND MOSSES, LICHENS, AND ALGAE BLANKET ITS BARK IN A GREY-GREEN SHROUD.

*R*OBUR, THE LATIN NAME FOR THE OAK, ALSO MEANT STRENGTH TO THE ROMANS. KNOWN FOR ITS HARDY, DURABLE WOOD, THIS TIMBER TREE CAN LIVE UP TO TWO OR THREE CENTURIES, PRODUCING MILLIONS OF ACORNS. THE DRUIDS PERFORMED A CEREMONY IN WHICH THEY CUT MISTLETOE FROM AN OAK WITH A SICKLE OF GOLD ON THE SIXTH DAY OF THE MOON. THE NAME OF THIS PAGAN RELIGION MAY IN FACT COMBINE DRUS, THE GREEK NAME FOR THE OAK, WITH THE INDO-EUROPEAN WID, MEANING TO KNOW.

*M*OST IMPORTANT OF THE TIMBER TREES, THE OAK YIELDS BEAUTIFULLY GRAINED WOOD IDEAL FOR FURNITURE AND FINISHING LUMBER. OTHER TREES MAKE A CONTRIBUTION AS WELL. FROM THE SOFT WOOD OF THE POPLAR COMES PAPER PULP AND FROM THE WALNUT COMES KNOTTY BURLWOOD FROM WHICH PIANOS ARE MADE. THE SAP-FILLED TWIGS OF THE BIRCH CAN BE BREWED INTO BIRCH BEER AND THE SAP OF THE MAPLE BOILED INTO MAPLE SYRUP. ALTHOUGH FAIRLY RARE SINCE THE BLIGHT OF 1904, THE CHESTNUT PRODUCES TANNING COMPOUNDS AS WELL AS WOOD FOR FURNITURE, FLAGPOLES, AND RAILROAD TIES.

TREE HOUSES ARE A CONFESSION OF OUR PRIMAL APE ANCESTRY.

"*It* WAS HIS OPINION THAT THIS LAND WAS DYING FOR WANT OF TREES. HE ADDED THAT, HAVING NO VERY PRESSING BUSINESS OF HIS OWN, HE HAD RESOLVED TO REMEDY THIS STATE OF AFFAIRS --- CREATION SEEMED TO COME ABOUT IN A SORT OF CHAIN REACTION --- THE WIND, TOO, SCATTERED SEEDS. AS THE WATER REAPPEARED, SO THERE REAPPEARED WILLOWS, RUSHES, MEADOWS, GARDENS, FLOWERS, AND A CERTAIN PURPOSE IN BEING ALIVE."

THE MAN WHO PLANTED TREES,
JEAN GIONO

Yellow Birch

Exotic Woods

Admired and used by humankind for thousands of years, exotic woods now face a serious threat from global deforestation.

Native to Burma, India, and Thailand, teak is highly prized for its extraordinary durability and beauty. The unseasoned heartwood has an alluring fragrance and a warm golden-yellow color, which seasons into a brown with dark streaks. Teak is rare because most of its seeds are sterile; forest fires wipe out a significant portion of those seeds which are fertilized.

Mahogany, a tropical hardwood, has a reddish brown hue that lends great splendor to furniture and paneling. Because mahogany is so rare and expensive, yellow birch is sometimes stained and used as a stand in.

If while wandering through Sri Lanka you come across a tree with charred-looking bark, you may just have found ebony. But you might be fooled by the color of the wood immediately under the bark. This layer, the cambium, is pure white. Only the heartwood is jet black.

Famous for its scent, sandalwood feeds in part on the roots of other tree species. Sandalwood is used to make furniture, fans, and boxes, sandalwood oil goes into perfumes, soaps, incense, candles, and folk medicines. In India, Brahman Hindus mark their skin with a paste made from powdered sandalwood, which is also used in sachets to scent clothing.

Cedar, perhaps the best known of the aromatic woods, frequently lines closets and chests, imparting a fresh, clean odor to heirloom tapestries and cherished clothing while protecting them from moths.

Red Cedar

Plants to Paper

Paper is nothing more than an amalgam of cellulose fiber derived from trees. Sometimes combined with cotton rag fiber, a pulpy mash of cellulose is rolled onto screens to dry into sheets of paper. A simple invention, but one that has changed the world.

Paper is communication. Probably originating in first-century China, it made its way around the globe from there. The nations and empires it reached recorded their history on its surface, preserving culture in portable form.

Paper is commerce. With the invention of paper currency, coins became obsolete. In the information age, many financial transactions take place only "on paper," without benefit of actual money.

Paper is literature and poetry.

Paper is art.

Flower petals

Giants of the Earth

Stringybark Gum
234'-301'

Port Orford Cedar
210'-225'

California Red Fir
177'-180'

Western White Pine
219'-240'

Perhaps the loftiest tree on earth, the tallest known redwood tree towers 367·8 feet into the air, 33 feet taller than the Statue of Liberty. The biggest sequoia in the world, known as the General Sherman, measures 272·4 feet tall and 101·6 feet around at its base, and weighs an estimated 12 million pounds. That weight includes about 750,000 pounds of roots and 14,000 pounds of bark. If it were cut for timber, the tree would yield about 600,120 board-feet of lumber – enough to build 40 five-room houses.

Although the best known, the coastal redwood and the giant sequoia are not the only giant trees on earth. Others include the Douglas fir, the Alaska cedar, and the Sitka spruce. Fossilized pine cones of giant trees date to the upper Jurassic period 130 million years ago. Some of California's living redwoods have been around an estimated 3,500 years.

For all its hugeness, the sequoia does not boast particularly strong wood. When these mighty trees fall, they usually splinter into useless fragments, leaving less than half the tree intact. Sequoias are no longer used for lumber, though some Native Americans, such as the Yurok of Northern California, once built their homes and canoes from its wood. Other indigenous peoples, including the Mono of the Sierra Nevadas, held the sequoia sacred and would not cut timber from it.

Giant Sequoia
273'-346'

Pacific Silver Fir
245'-268'

Eastern White Pine
161'-220'

Southern Blue Gum
261'-350'

Coast Redwood
368'-394'

Swamp Gum
234'-301'

Sugar Pine
240'-270'

White Pine
151'-205'

Sitka Spruce
224'-295'

Grand Fir
185'-298'

White Fir
189'-194'

American Elm
164'-180'

Corsican Pine
164'-180'

$\mathcal{S}$URPRISINGLY, THE
ROOTS OF GIANT TREES REACH ONLY
FOUR TO SIX FEET INTO THE SOIL.
HOWEVER, THEY EXTEND AN AVERAGE OF
40 TO 50 FEET FROM THE BASE OF THE
TREE AND CAN COVER MORE
THAN AN ACRE IF CONDITIONS
ARE DRY. AS WATER
EVAPORATES FROM THE LEAVES AT THE TOP OF THE TREE,
WATER IS DRAWN INTO THE ROOTS AT THE BOTTOM AND FROM THERE
INTO THE XYLEM, WHICH ACTS AS A GIANT STRAW. GIANT TREES
EXERT SUCH TREMENDOUS VACUUM PRESSURE THAT THE
XYLEM CAN CRACK DURING DRY SEASONS, WHEN
IT BECOMES BRITTLE.

$\mathcal{T}$HE SEEDS OF THE COASTAL
REDWOOD ARE AS TINY AS THE TREE IS LARGE, WEIGHING
IN AT ABOUT 123,000 PER POUND. ONE TREE MIGHT PRODUCE
FIVE MILLION SEEDS IN A YEAR, BUT MOST OF THEM NEVER
PENETRATE THE THICK GROUND COVER. WHEN FOREST FIRES
BURN OFF THE CARPET OF DECAYING LEAVES AND FERNS,
THE SEEDS CAN REACH SOIL AND GERMINATE.

Coastal Redwood

Douglas Fir
302'-417'

Norway Spruce
180'-200'

Ponderosa Pine
180'-246'

Western Red Cedar
140'-200'

Dawn Redwood
115'-140'

Noble Fir
260'-260'

"PECANS ARE A CHOICE INGREDIENT OF BOTH FRUITCAKES AND SQUIRRELS. SOME TEN MILLION POUNDS ARE INCORPORATED ANNUALLY INTO EACH. IN FRUITCAKES, PECANS IMPROVE THE COLOR, TEXTURE AND TASTE ... IN SQUIRRELS, NUTS ARE VITAL. A DIET OF PECANS, WITH THEIR SEVENTY PERCENT OIL CONTENT, IS RESPONSIBLE FOR A HIGHER BIRTHRATE ..."

EARTHLY PLEASURES: TALES FROM A
BIOLOGIST'S GARDEN, ROGER B. SWAIN, 1981

TECHNICALLY, A NUT IS A ONE-CELLED FRUIT ENVELOPED BY A DRY SHELL, SUCH AS THE ACORN, CHESTNUT, AND HAZELNUT. OFTEN, THE TERM IS ALSO APPLIED TO SEEDS OR EDIBLE FRUIT KERNELS ENCLOSED IN A HARD SHELL, SUCH AS THE ALMOND, CASHEW, AND WALNUT.

CRAZY ABOUT NUTS! EACH AUTUMN, TREE-DWELLING SQUIRRELS BECOME TRUE WORKAHOLICS, COLLECTING AND BURYING ACORNS WITH A FEROCIOUS URGENCY. THE BUSY RODENTS OFTEN FORGET WHERE THEY HAVE HIDDEN THEIR STOCKPILES, ALLOWING THE NUTS TO GERMINATE INTO OAK SEEDLINGS. HUMANS, TOO, HAVE ENJOYED THE FLAVOR OF ACORNS. SOME HISTORIANS SUGGEST THAT IN ITS RELATIVELY BRIEF HISTORY, HUMANKIND MAY HAVE CONSUMED MORE ACORNS THAN WHEAT.

Brazil Nut

IN A NUTSHELL

ACTUALLY THE SEED OF AN AMAZONIAN TREE, BRAZIL NUTS COME FROM A FRUIT THAT WEIGHS UP TO FOUR AND A HALF POUNDS. WITHIN ITS THICK, WOODY SHELL, THE FRUIT CONTAINS ONE OR TWO DOZEN SEEDS ARRANGED IN ORANGE-LIKE SECTIONS. HEADS UP WHEN THIS FRUIT FALLS!

THE NUTCRACKER, A BIRD FOUND IN CONIFEROUS FORESTS, HELPS PLANT LIFE REPRODUCE BY EATING NUTS AND SEEDS THAT IT LATER REGURGITATES AND BURIES FOR WINTER USE.

Clark's Nutcracker

IN MEDIEVAL EUROPE, DINERS SWALLOWED WHOLE WALNUTS AT THE END OF A MEAL, BELIEVING THE NUT WORKED AS A SORT OF CORK OR STOMACH STOPPER TO AID DIGESTION.

WINTER RITUALS: PASSED FROM HAND TO HAND BEFORE A COZY FIRE, A BOWL OF NUTS AND A NUTCRACKER BRINGS A CIRCLE OF FRIENDS TOGETHER. THE NUTCRACKER THAT COMES TO LIFE IN TCHAIKOVSKY'S NUTCRACKER SUITE BECOMES THE STUFF OF SUGARPLUM DREAMS AND SNOWFLAKE MEMORIES FOR CHILDREN AT CHRISTMASTIME.

Forest Facts

Chanterelle

Earthball

Death Cap

THICK FORESTS ONCE COVERED LARGE AREAS OF THE NORTHERN HEMISPERE'S TEMPERATE ZONE, WHERE THE DENSEST HUMAN POPULATIONS NOW LIVE. DIFFERING ACCORDING TO LOCAL CONDITIONS, MOST OF THE REMAINING WOODLANDS ARE A MOSAIC OF COMMUNITIES DOMINATED BY DECIDUOUS BROADLEAF TREE SPECIES SUCH AS OAK, BEECH, AND MAPLE.

THE OPENINGS IN THE TEMPERATE FOREST CANOPY ALLOW SMALLER PLANTS TO FLOURISH ON THE WOODLAND FLOOR. THE DELIRIUM OF FLOWERS THAT CARPETS THE GROUND IN SPRING SURVIVES THE WINTER AS BULBS, CORMS, OR RHIZOMES. IN AUTUMN, FALLEN LEAVES DECOMPOSE RAPIDLY WITH THE HELP OF VARIOUS FUNGI, CREATING RICH SOIL FOR THE GROWTH OF THE FOLLOWING SPRING. UNFORTUNATELY, THE HUMAN APPETITE FOR FERTILE FARMLAND AND FRESH TIMBER HAS RESULTED IN EXTENSIVE CLEARCUTTING OF THE FOREST.

PEOPLE USED TO THINK MUSHROOMS POPPED OUT OF THE GROUND BY MAGIC. IN FACT, THE REAL MAGIC OF MUSHROOMS IS THAT WHAT WE SEE ABOVE GROUND IS ONLY THE TIP OF THE FUNGAL ICEBERG. THE MUSHROOM CAP OF THE FAMILIAR TOADSTOOL IS ITS FRUITING BODY. WHEN RIPE, THE GILLS ON THE UNDERSIDE CAN PRODUCE AT LEAST 100,000 SPORES TO BE RELEASED IN A DUSTY GUST. BUT THE MUSHROOM DOES ITS REAL WORK IN SECRET UNDERGROUND.

Thick-Footed Morel

Sweet Tooth

Black Truffle

Yellow Morel

Meadow Mushroom

Shaggy Mane

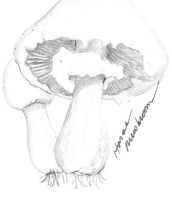
Horse Mushroom

Bitter Bolete

BENEATH THE SOIL, GERMINATING MUSHROOM SPORES GROW LITTLE TUBES KNOWN AS HYPHAE, WHICH BRANCH OUT AND JOIN WITH THE HYPHAE OF OTHER SPORES. THE RESULTING WHITE MASS OF FILAMENTS IS CALLED THE MYCELIUM. IN AS LITTLE AS EIGHT HOURS AFTER GERMINATION, LITTLE KNOBS APPEAR ON THE MYCELIUM AND PUSH TOWARDS THE SURFACE OF THE EARTH TO FEED ON ORGANIC DEBRIS. WERE IT NOT FOR THE SILENT EFFICIENCY OF THE FUNGUS, THE EARTH WOULD SMOTHER UNDER ITS OWN WASTE.

AMONG THE WORLD'S FABULOUS FUNGI, TRUFFLES FULFILL MANY CULINARY FANTASIES. TO FEMALE BOARS, HOWEVER, THEY HOLD ALL THE FRUSTRATIONS OF UNREQUITED LOVE. IN ONE OF ITS CRUELER TRICKS, NATURE HAS ENDOWED TRUFFLES WITH A PHEROMONE ALMOST IDENTICAL TO THE ONE RELEASED BY MALE BOARS IN MATING SEASON. HUMAN TRUFFLE HUNTERS HAVE LEARNED TO EXPLOIT THE SOW'S PASSION BY SENDING HER INTO THE FOREST TO FIND THE SOURCE OF THE SEXY SCENT. DIGGING FRANTICALLY AT THE BASE OF A TREE, THE SOW UNEARTHS AND ABANDONS TRUFFLES, CONTINUING HER SEARCH WITH SNOUT AQUIVER.

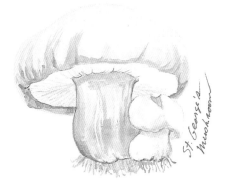
St. George's Mushroom

Black Morel

Fly Agaric

"Lovely! see the cloud appear!

Lovely! See the rain, the rain draw near!

Who spoke?

It was the little corn ear

high on the tip of the stalk."

TRADITIONAL ZUÑI CORN-GRINDING SONG

Wetland

Wet and Wild

Wetland habitats include marshes, bogs, fens, swamps, mires, saltmarshes, mangrove swamps, estuaries, prairie potholes, lakes, and rivers. Evolutionary rest-stops for life-forms migrating from aquatic to terrestrial homes, these ecosystems remain some of the earth's most productive biomes. They compare to rainforests as breeding grounds and nurseries for countless plant, insect, bird, and other animal species.

Growing as they do at least partially submerged, wetland plants have air spaces inside their stems, leaves, and roots to provide bouyancy and aid in the exchange of gases. Unlikely to dehydrate, the underwater parts have no waterproofing; they also lack some of the support structures found in land plants, as they spend their lives floating in an easy water ballet.

Making a forest on stilts, mangroves in tropical tidal waters grow into self-repairing coastal flood barriers. Crustaceans and waterfowl flock to the swamps to feed and mate, just as children flock to marshes in search of cattails. Breaking open the brown velveteen tails that wag atop six-foot stems, they love to blow the fluffy seeds away on the breeze.

Waterlogged bogs support carnivorous plants and acid-lovers such as cotton grasses, sedge, and "drunken forests" of leaning birch, alder, pine, and spruce. The peatlands known as pocosins, from the Algonquin word meaning "swamp-on-a-hill," are situated on flat land between two rivers. They support spiny vegetation that provides a refuge for black bears and bobcats.

Nenuphar, the french name for the water lily, may have come from the latin Nymphaea, the source of the english Nymph. Perhaps taken with the connection, impressionist painter Claude Monet entitled his series of huge water lily canvases Les Nymphaeas. The floral fairies in the pond he built in his garden at Giverny emerged from the water at sunrise and re-entered at sunset.

In the amazon waters of Manaus, Brazil, the gigantic Regalia Lily grows up to six feet in diameter. Its luxurious blossoms boast hundreds of petals in shades from white to pink to rose. Vegetable stepping-stones for frogs who seek a courting platform or a route across the water, its majestic leaves feature prominent inch-high ribs. So sturdy are they that they can easily support the weight of a slumbering human infant.

Rainforest

Giant Himalayan Lily

It's a Jungle Out There

The deep, dark jungles of our imagination are embellished versions of the complex and varied biomes encompassed by the rainforest. Warm and wet as bath water, these evergreen expanses enjoy an endless growing season. Tropical rainforests cover only 6% of the earth's surface, but they contain more than half the world's known species of flora and fauna.

In the humid climate of the Costa Rican cloud forest, there may be fewer than ten clear, cloudless days a year.

Beneath an almost unbroken roof of leaves, the rainforest boasts a great diversity of habitats and several distinct layers of foliage. The canopy, formed by the large spreading crowns of the tallest trees, extends over the entire forest and keeps most of its denizens in perpetual shade.

Low-growing, shrub-like species crowd the dim rainforest floor, their growth limited by the lack of light. In the damp and murk, moss, lichen, and ferns overgrow stunted trees, while spiny rattan and climbing palms thrust their tendrils toward the feeble light. Vines, lianas, and other trailing plants twine around tree trunks.

Fungi abound in the world of the rainforest, which seems made just for them. A constant deadfall of plant and animal matter drops to the forest floor, where fungi transform it into soil. This sole source of nutrients for the naturally poor soil is eliminated when a patch of tropical forest is cut down.

Uninformed developers deceived by the teeming rainforest clearcut the trees in order to plant commercial crops or create grazing lands for livestock. But within a few years, the unreplenished land is exhausted, and the soil, unprotected by any root system, has eroded.

Survival

Perhaps the notion of divine resurrection was inspired by plants, for, faced with the worst privations of nature or humankind, many ravaged plants can rise again. Pruned roses bloom season after season; fruit trees unfurl twice their original number of branches.

Don't touch me! An armory of thorns, spikes, and barbs keep plant enemies at bay. To keep birds from perching on it and animals from stealing its water supplies, the Cholla Cactus sports the ultimate in thorns. The bristly hairs on the stem of the hemp nettle make climbing difficult for invading insects, while the thorn apple protects its seeds with thorns and a toxic chemical in the seed coat.

The foxglove plant warns away animals with its acrid smell. Those who don't take the hint are poisoned if they eat any part of the plant; large doses of foxglove can cause cardiac arrest.

Poison ivy, the campers' scourge, defends itself with an irritating contact poison that produces a mighty itch on the skin of all who touch it.

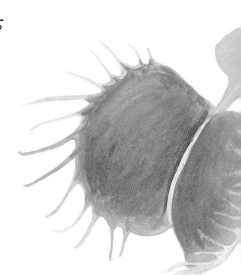

Using Bright Colors And Heady Nectar To Lure Prey, Carnivorous Plants Supplement Their Photosynthetic Diet By Feeding On Insects. The Venus Fly Trap, Pitcher Plant, And Butterwort Trap And Eat Ants, Flies, Gnats, Worms, Dragonflies, And Even Small Frogs.

Set Off By An Alighting Victim, Trigger Hairs On The Venus Fly Trap Slam Its Hinged Leaf Lobes Shut. Inside, The Prey Is Dissolved By Digestive Enzymes.

The Pitcher Plant's Slippery Surface Sends Insects Sliding Into A Pool Of Liquid Deep Inside, Where They Slowly Decompose.

Palms

More than 2,600 species of palms vary in size, leaf type, flower type, and fruit yield. Creatures of comfort, palms thrive in the tropics. Only a few live in subtropical areas such as Southern California and Florida, and only one species, the Trachycarpus Fortunei, or Windmill Palm, of the Far East, can tolerate snow and ice.

Regardless of species, palms always lack branches and annual rings. Sprouting from the top of the trunk, palm fronds are actually leaves made up of discrete leaflet segments. The four types of palm leaves can grow up to 15 feet in length. Fan leaves feature broad leaflets radiating out from a point on the center rib, while modified fan leaves have shorter, thinner leaflets. The broad leaflets of cabbage leaves grow all along the center rib, as do the whispy, thin leaflets of feather leaves.

A palm's leaves grow from an all-important bud perched atop the trunk of the tree. Unfortunately, it is a tasty bud that animals (and humans) like to eat. The tree protects itself with spikes along its trunk, although palms on remote islands have evolved none because they do not need protection.

EACH PALM TREE HAS A SPECIFIC GENDER, SO IT RELIES ON INSECTS AND BREEZES TO CARRY POLLEN TO OR FROM OTHER TREES. POLLINATION PRODUCES THE COCONUT, BELIEVED TO BE THE WORLD'S LARGEST SEED. THE BOUYANT, WATERPROOF SEED IS OFTEN TRANSPORTED TO FAR-OFF BEACHES BY THE SEA. WITH ITS HAIRY, BROWN SHELL AND THREE "EYES," THE COCONUT RESEMBLES A MONKEY'S FACE. THE SEED EARNED ITS NAME FROM COCOS, THE PORTUGUESE WORD FOR MONKEY.

HUMAN USES FOR THE PALM ARE ENDLESS. RAFFIA, A FIBER USED TO MAKE BASKETS AND MATS, COMES FROM THE LEAF STALKS OF THE VINE PALM. THE DENIZENS OF TROPICAL ASIA CHEW THE SEEDS OF THE BETEL NUT PALM MIXED WITH PEPPER LEAVES. IN INDIA, THE PALMYRA PALM YIELDS PALM WINE, AND THE SUGAR PALM YIELDS PALM SUGAR. PALM OIL COMES FROM THE AFRICAN OIL PALM, WHILE BEAUTIFUL BUTTONS CAN BE MADE FROM THE "VEGETABLE IVORY" OF THE BRAZILIAN IVORY PALM. SOME BELIEVE THAT CHEWING PALM LEAVES CAN RELIEVE A FEVER.

IN SOME CULTURES, PALMS ARE BELIEVED TO HAVE SPECIAL POWERS. CARRIED OR WORN, A PIECE OF PALM WOOD OR A PALM LEAF IS SAID TO SUBDUE EVIL SPIRITS. IT IS ALSO SUGGESTED THAT A CROSS MADE OF PALM LEAVES KEEPS LIGHTNING AWAY. AND IF YOU DREAM OF A FLOWERING PALM TREE, LUCK AND SUCCESS MAY BE YOURS IN THE FUTURE.

BAMBOO

Lanky, Lissome Bamboo

The simple beauty of bamboo is matched by its incredible resilience. Flexible but tough, light yet strong, the plant can survive monsoons and hurricanes. In earthquake-prone Japan, intricate bamboo root systems stabilize the earth.

首日封 F.D.C.

Each of the approximately 1,250 species of bamboo has one or two root systems. Tropical varieties, known as sympodial, or clumping, bamboo, sprout underground shoots called rhizomes, which grow upward into new culms (stems). In cooler climates, the rhizomes of monopodial or free-standing bamboo species tunnel deep into the earth. Buds that sprout from joints or nodes along the length of the rhizome grow to the surface to become new plants.

Bamboo reaches maturity in less than a year, accomplishing most of its growth in the space of two months. Gaining as much as four feet of height in a day, bamboo can be seen and sometimes heard growing. As it stretches upward, it lets loose a deep-throated creeeeeeeak.

Some species of bamboo live up to 120 years. The flowering of a bamboo plant is a sad moment for the bamboo farmer, for the plant blooms just before death. All over the world, dying bamboo plants of the same species flower simultaneously.

A Japanese legend tells of the princess Kaguyahime, who was found inside a bamboo culm by a poor and childless farmer. The little girl grew into a great beauty and was pursued by many suitors, including the emperor himself. But Kaguyahime declared she would never marry. When angels came down from the full moon and carried her there, she left behind a letter to the emperor. He had it burned at the top of the highest mountain in the land. Because the smoke lingered about the peak, the mountain came to be known as Fuji, the immortal one.

At night, Asian travelers camped in the wilderness tied stalks of green bamboo together and suspended their bundles over their campfires. As the wood slowly blistered and burned, it intermittently exploded, frightening away dangerous beasts.

Among bamboo's many uses, some of the more curious are bamboo organ pipes and gramophone needles. Thomas Edison used bamboo for the filaments in his first electric lamps.

Dryland

High and dry

Although naturalists regard true wilderness as those areas that remain completely untouched by human hands, hikers in uninhabited country accessible only by trail can experience the vast splendor and volatile temperament of mother nature. Their trek will be especially rewarding if they follow the desert siren.

$\mathcal{D}$ESERTS ARE NOT NECESSARILY HOT PLACES. FOR INSTANCE, THE GOBI DESERT IN CENTRAL ASIA AND THE ATACAMA DESERT OF CHILE ARE BOTH COOL. IT IS THE ABSENCE OF RAIN, SOMETIMES FOR YEARS AT A TIME, THAT DEFINES THESE BIOMES. PLANTS THRIVING HERE OFTEN SURVIVE ON ONLY THE MOISTURE CREATED BY THE CONDENSATION OF THE NIGHT AIR INTO DEW.

$\mathcal{I}$N EFFECT, POLAR REGIONS ARE DESERTS, BECAUSE THE PRECIPITATION THAT FALLS THERE REMAINS FROZEN AND CANNOT BE USED BY PLANTS OR ANIMALS. BASED UPON A VERY THIN LAYER OF SOIL, THE ARCTIC TUNDRA IS A VAST EXPANSE OF SHRUBBY VEGETATION. LONG-LIVED CUSHION PLANTS GROW BENEATH A BLANKET OF SNOW, WHICH ACTUALLY INSULATES THEM. LICHENS AND MOSS, WHICH COVER LESS THAN 20% OF THE GROUND AT CANADA'S POLAR BEAR PASS, SUSTAIN LARGE HERDS OF MIGRATING CARIBOU.

$\mathcal{D}$ESERT PLANTS IN HOT REGIONS BOAST EXTENSIVE ROOT SYSTEMS AND REDUCED LEAF AREAS TO MINIMIZE WATER LOSS. THEIR THICK SKIN ACTS AS A WATERPROOF COATING THAT LOCKS IN MOISTURE. LIKE MANY CACTI, THE CENTURY PLANT HAS SUNKEN STOMAS OR PORES, TO REDUCE EVAPORATION. ANOTHER WATER-SAVING DEVICE IS THE RIDGE-AND-CHANNEL SURFACE OF THE SAGUARO CACTUS, WHICH CAN STORE UP TO TEN GALLONS OF WATER IN ITS SUCCULENT, BULBOUS SHOOTS. THE TAMARISK PLANT, MEANWHILE, SECRETES A SOLUTION OF CALCIUM CHLORIDE FROM ITS LEAVES TO ATTRACT AND ABSORB MOISTURE.

FLOWER

"Earth laughs in flowers."

— RALPH WALDO EMERSON

The body plan of a flower

The most widespread and successful form of plant life, the angiosperms, possess true flower power. Their flowers perform the critical task of producing seeds in order to perpetuate the species.

The flower, one of nature's most exuberant accomplishments, is painstakingly designed to fulfill its reproductive purpose. Many flowers contain both male stamens and female pistils. The threadlike stalks of the stamens support sack-like, pollen-producing anthers, while the pollen-receiving pistil normally has a stigma, a stile, and an ovary. Often sticky, the stigma traps pollen grains that touch it. Pollen travels down the neck-like style to the ovary, where it fertilizes the egg cells. After fertilization, the ovary matures into a fruit that helps protect the seeds.

Since floral sex is a proxy affair, the arts of enticement are directed solely at the go-betweens who transport pollen from flower to flower. To these insect and animal intermediaries, flowers offer the seductive enchantments of color, perfume, pollen, and nectar.

Chiropterophilic (literally, bat-loving) plants are pollinated by nectar-feeding bats. Open at night, their flowers have a pale or reddish color and a strong scent that often resembles the odor of fermenting fruit. Agave flowers remain open for several nights, switching from the production of pollen to the production of nectar. This strategy minimizes the chances of self-fertilization and attracts repeated visits from pollen-carrying bats.

PATTERNS, STRIPES, SPECKLES, AND SWATCHES OF COLOR SERVE
AS FIELD GUIDES TO INSECT LANDING STRIPS.

WHITE CAMPION, STOCK, AND EVENING PRIMROSE
FILL THE NIGHT AIR WITH AN IRRESISTIBLE PERFUME
TO LURE MOTHS SEARCHING FOR SUPPER. THESE
FLOWERS ARE MODESTLY
ATTIRED IN DELICATE WHITES
AND CHASTE PASTELS, AS
MORE VIBRANT COLORS
WOULD BE WASTED IN
THE DARK.

ONLY BUTTERFLIES
AND MOTHS WITH LONG
PROBOSCISES CAN SIP
THE NECTAR FROM
THE NARROW CALYX
OF THE HONEYSUCKLE.

EACH SPECIES
OF FIG DEPENDS
ON A SINGLE
VARIETY OF
WASP FOR
POLLINATION.
NO WASPS,
NO FIGS.

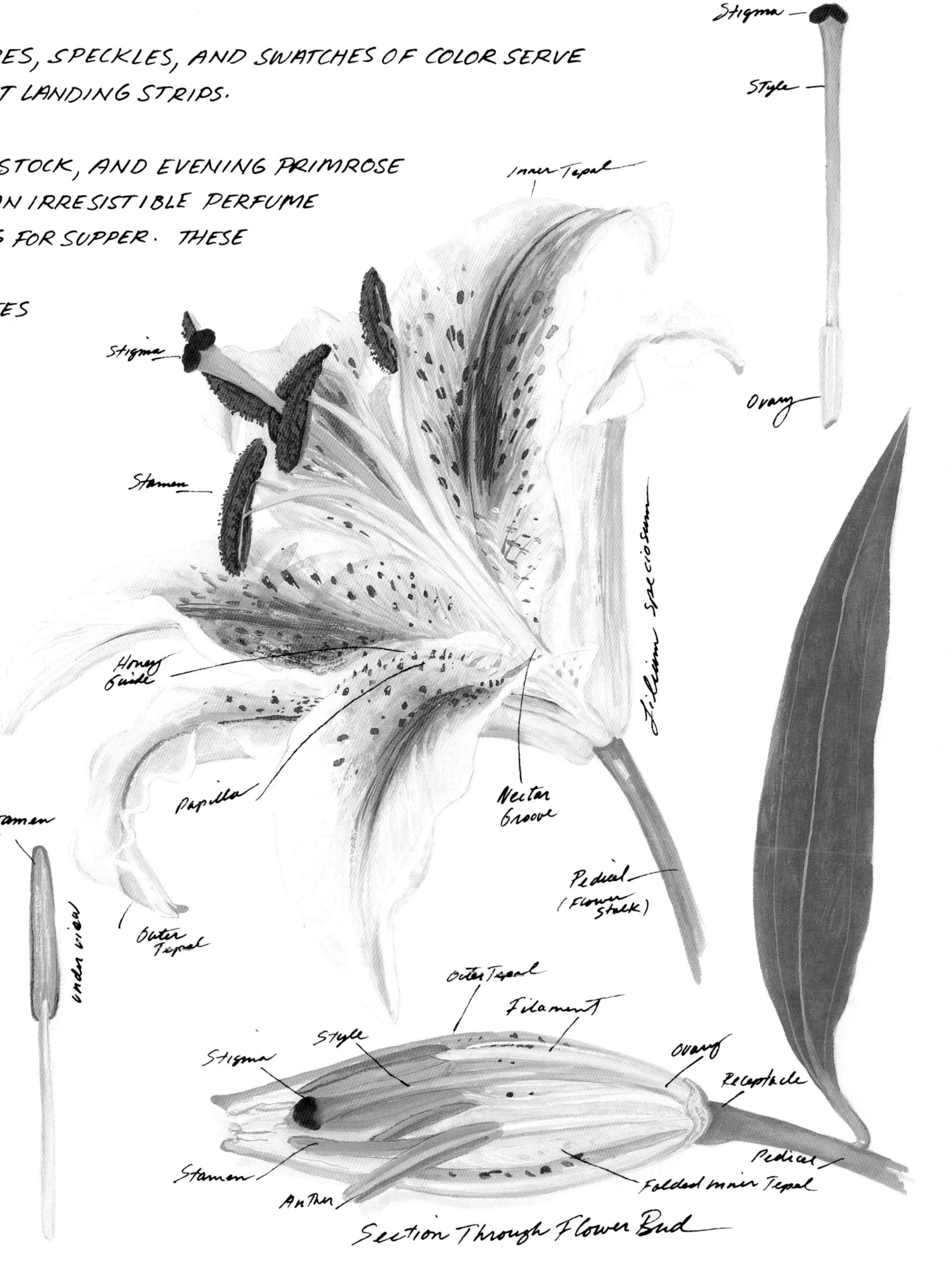

Stigma

Style

Inner Tepal

Ovary

Stigma

Stamen

Lilium speciosum

Honey Guide

Papilla

Nectar Groove

Pedical (Flower Stalk)

Stamen

Top View

Under view

Anther

Filament

Outer Tepal

Outer Tepal

Filament

Style

Stigma

Ovary

Receptacle

Stamen

Anther

Folded inner Tepal

Pedical

Section Through Flower Bud

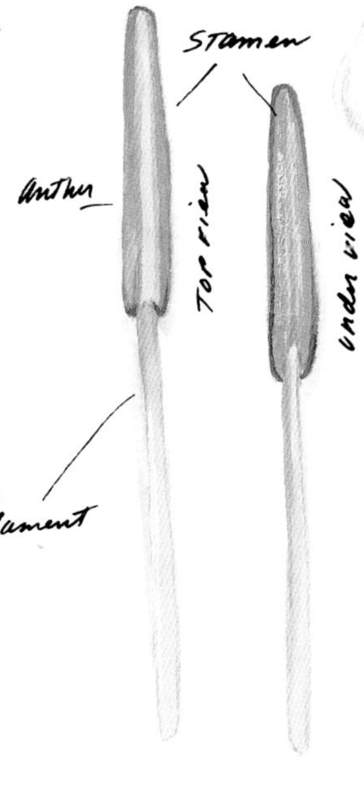

Madonna Lily

Parrot Tulip

Violet

Forget-me-Not

Jasmine

Pansy

Climbing Rose

Daphne

Primrose

Hardenbergia
Violacea

Iris

Rosemary

Gloriosa Lily

Delphinium

Orchid

Camelia

Hydrangea

Paris Daisy

Almond Blossom

Shrub Rose

Orchid

Freesia

Nosegay to Bouquet

Bravo! to wild applause, a bouquet of flowers is thrown at the feet of the opera diva, actor, or prima ballerina. The culmination of nature's virtuosity, flowers are a fitting tribute of extravagant praise, approval, love, and gratitude.

A little post-victorian book, The Language of Flowers, listed more than 700 blooms and their significance. In the age of chaperones, a nosegay could be arranged in a secret code and presented to the beloved to speak volumes in a passion of petals. The rose alone expresses 40 different sentiments: those in the know can reproach a friend, quarrel, and make up without inking their fingers or raising their voice.

Anything that will hold water: take a cue from nature's fertile imagination and freely mix-and-match plants and flowers in any good excuse for a container. An old mason jar in a boot will do, with ivy shoelaces and sunflower socks. Put fresh peppercorns in a red pepperbox.

Ikebana, the Japanese art of floral arrangement, reflects the meditative, philosophical, and poetic elements of Buddhism. Brought to Japan by Chinese missionaries in the 6th century, Buddhist practices included the use of flowers in ritual offerings. In the 7th century, Ono No Imoko established Ikenobo, the first Japanese school of flower arranging. His approach emphasized the harmony of simple linear construction, the use of natural materials, and an appreciation of the subtle beauty of flowers. Several major schools of Ikebana later developed, differentiated by their historical influences, their artistic theories, and the individual styles of their founders.

PEPPERMINT - WARMTH
PANSY - THOUGHTS
PURPLE LILAC - FIRST EMOTIONS OF LOVE
ROSE - LOVE
FORGET-ME-NOT - TRUE LOVE

LIGHT

"LET THERE BE LIGHT...

LET THE WATERS BE GATHERED TOGETHER IN ONE PLACE

AND LET THE DRY LAND APPEAR...

LET THE EARTH BRING FORTH GRASS, THE HERB YIELDING SEED,

AND THE FRUIT TREE YIELDING FRUIT."

GENESIS 1:3, 9, 11

Solar snacks

The key to all life on earth is a process that takes but a fraction of a second. Photosynthesis, the first link in the global food chain, is the complex mechanism by which plants make their food from sunlight.

Plants trap the sun in a substance called chlorophyll, carried in pellet-shaped leaf structures called chloroplasts. Twisting and jostling on their stems, leaves maximize their exposure for solar energy collection.

When light strikes the surface of a leaf, it flicks the "on" switch of the organic food factory that manufactures simple sugars. In less than one one-hundredth of a second, a photosynthesizing plant performs up to a hundred different but interconnected chemical changes.

Drawing water up from its roots and inhaling carbon dioxide through the pores on its leaves, a plant uses chlorophyll to combine these components into basic carbohydrates. These sugars are later converted into more complex sugars, starches, proteins, and fats.

The astonishing process ends with a great green sigh as the plant exhales the unnecessary by-product, oxygen, into the atmosphere.

Think about it:
If you munch a freshly-picked leaf during daylight hours, you are eating the sun.

No man can harvest sunbeams~ but a dandelion can.

Sunflower

Exemplifying the phenomenon of compound inflorescence, the sunflower contains hundreds of flowers within one huge blossom. Each of the individual "florets" has its own ovary, stigma, style, and anthers and produces a single seed. Sunflower blossoms can grow to enormous proportions — the largest on record had a circumference of 52½ inches. Sometimes a sunflower's stalk can't support the weight of the huge flower, causing the plant to bend or topple over.

Startlingly lovely, these ocher giants are also valuable. Their leaves are used as animal fodder, their flowers yield a yellow dye, their seeds are nutritious, and oil extracted from the seeds can be used in food, soap, and paint.

The house that sunflowers built: to create a floral retreat, plant two parallel rows of sunflowers. Thread string from the flower heads in one row to those in the other, then plant morning glories at their base. The eager blue glories will loop their way up the sunflower stems and across the string, forming a majestic canopy under which to lie.

Vincent van Gogh, the 19th-century Dutch painter, created a series of bold, moody sunflower portraits. Although he died a pauper, one of these paintings sold in 1987 for a record $39.9 million.

Sunflowers got their name because the blossoms actually follow the sun's course across the sky. Chemicals in the phototropic plant's flowers are attracted to the sun's rays.

Violet Toilet Water

A GENUINE DELICATE, FRAGRANT AND LASTING ODOR OF NATURAL VIOLET FLOWERS

WM. SMITH & CO.

Fragona

GRASSE-PARIS-ÈZ

VISITEZ NOS USINE

PARFUMER

A CHEMICAL ATTRACTION

"VIOLETS SMELL LIKE BURNT SUGAR CUBES THAT HAVE BEEN DIPPED IN LEMON AND VELVET."

A NATURAL HISTORY OF THE SENSES, DIANE ACKERMAN, 1991

THE FLARE OF PRIMAL REACTION DETONATED BY THE FRAGRANCE OF CERTAIN FLOWERS AND HERBS OVERWHELMS ALL OUR SENSES. RELEASED BY PLANTS HOPING TO ATTRACT INSECT AND ANIMAL POLLINATORS, MICROSCOPIC BOMBS OF FRAGRANT CHEMICALS FLOAT THROUGH THE AIR IN SEARCH OF A TARGET. THE EXPLOSION OF SMELL HITS US RIGHT IN THE NOSE, THEN MELTS OR RACES THROUGH OUR ENTIRE SENSORY SYSTEM.

18th Century Islamic Perfume Bottle

20th Century French Perfume Bottle

AZUREA

L.T. PIVER
PARIS

$\mathcal{V}$IOLETS PLAY HARD TO GET WITH THEIR NOW-YOU-SMELL-IT, NOW-YOU-DON'T AROMA. THEY OWE THEIR EPHEMERAL SCENT TO THE CHEMICAL IONONE, WHICH PROJECTS AN INTENSE SWEETNESS THAT WAXES AND WANES FROM ONE MOMENT TO THE NEXT. VIOLET PERFUME GIVES ITS WEARER A FRAGRANCE - AND AN AURA - THAT'S HARD TO PIN DOWN.

$\mathcal{C}$LEOPATRA'S SCENTED STRATEGY: IT SEEMS AT LEAST ONE ROMAN LEADER WAS DEFEATED BY A NOSE. ON A VISIT TO MARK ANTONY, CLEOPATRA SUPPOSEDLY ARRIVED ON A CEDAR SHIP WITH SAILS PERFUMED BY INCENSE BURNERS. SHE ANOINTED HER HANDS WITH KYPHI, AN OIL CONTAINING THE ESSENCE OF ROSES, CROCUS, AND VIOLETS, AND HER FEET WITH A LOTION OF ALMOND OIL, HONEY, CINNAMON, ORANGE BLOSSOMS, AND HENNA. THE EGYPTIAN QUEEN WAS SAID TO RECEIVE MARK ANTONY IN PRIVATE CHAMBERS STREWN WITH ROSE PETALS A FOOT AND HALF DEEP. HIS PASSION FOR CLEOPATRA WAS THE WARRIOR'S ULTIMATE DOWNFALL.

$\mathcal{A}$RGUABLY THE FIRST NOVEL EVER WRITTEN, THE TALE OF GENJI WAS WRITTEN BY LADY MURASAKI SHIKIBU IN 1006. THE SUBTLE SPLENDOR OF THESE TALES OF FEUDAL JAPAN IS HIGHLIGHTED BY DESCRIPTIONS OF THE COURT AND ITS AROMATIC CUSTOMS. IN A PERFUME COMPETITION, GENJI, THE HERO, EXPERIMENTS RAPTUROUSLY WITH EXTRACTS FROM PLANTS AND FLOWERS CULTIVATED EXPRESSLY FOR THIS PURPOSE.

ROSES

Rose Hips

"*I KNOW A BANK WHERE THE WILD THYME BLOWS,
WHERE OXLIPS AND THE NODDING VIOLET GROWS,
QUITE OVER-CANOPIED WITH LUSCIOUS WOODBINE,
WITH SWEET MUSK-ROSES, AND WITH EGLANTINE.*"

A MIDSUMMER NIGHT'S DREAM,
WILLIAM SHAKESPEARE 1594

*THE ROMAN EMPEROR
NERO SPENT THE EQUIVALENT
OF $16,000 ON ROSES FOR
A SINGLE BANQUET
CELEBRATING THE ROSALIA,
THE FESTIVAL OF ROSES. HIS
GUESTS ATE ROSE
PUDDINGS, BREATHED AIR
SCENTED WITH ROSE OIL,
AND RECLINED ON
PILLOWS STUFFED WITH
ROSE PETALS.*

Ga être
Poésie

GROWING SINGLY OR IN SMALL CLUSTERS, ROSES FEATURE FEATHER-SHAPED LEAVES, A THORNY STEM, AND USUALLY FIVE PETALS PER FLOWER, ALTHOUGH CULTIVATED VARIETIES OFTEN HAVE TWICE AS MANY. THE MOST COMMON SHADES ARE WHITE, YELLOW, ORANGE, PINK, AND RED; THERE HAS NEVER BEEN A BLUE ROSE, FOR ROSES LACK THE PIGMENT DELPHINIDIN. A PERENNIAL ANGIOSPERM, THE ROSE IS RELATED TO APPLES, CHERRIES, ORANGES, GRAPES, AND OTHER FRUITS. ITS FRUIT IS THE FLORAL CUP, WHICH IS KNOWN AS THE HIP, AND IS RICH IN VITAMIN C. DURING WORLD WAR II, ROSE HIPS HELPED PREVENT SCURVY IN GREAT BRITAIN, FILLING THE GAP LEFT BY A SCARCITY OF CITRUS FRUITS.

A PASSION FOR ROSES CAN OVERCOME ALL OBSTACLES. FIGHTING BETWEEN FRANCE AND ENGLAND DID NOT STOP EMPRESS JOSÉPHINE, WIFE OF NAPOLÉON I, FROM ENJOYING HER FAVORITE FLOWER. ENGLISH NURSERYMAN JOHN KENNEDY WAS PERMITTED PASSAGE ACROSS THE CHANNEL TO DELIVER GREAT QUANTITIES OF ROSES TO HER.

THOUGH NOT AS COSTLY AS RAISING ORCHIDS, CULTIVATING ROSES CAN PROVE A FORMIDABLE EXPENSE. ASKED HOW HE AFFORDED NEW AND COSTLY VARIETIES, AN ENGLISH WORKINGMAN REPLIED, "BY KEEPING AWAY FROM THE BEERSHOPS!"

A TIP FOR THE GARDENER: PLANT A FEW CLOVES OF GARLIC BESIDE A ROSEBUSH TO KEEP APHIDS AWAY. THE GARLIC WON'T AFFECT THE AROMA OF THE ROSE.

IT TAKES 11,000 POUNDS OF ROSE PETALS TO PRODUCE TWO POUNDS OF ROSE OIL.

*N*amed for its jagged leaves, which resemble lion's teeth, the dandelion is cursed by gardeners as a savage weed. Children, however, love its cheerful yellow flowers and its fluffy globes of wish-seeds.

*B*ecause some species of the daisy close their blossoms at night, it gained the old English name daeges eage, meaning "day's eye." The moniker eventually evolved into daisy.

*T*he brilliant orange flower in your salad tastes as spicy as it looks. The nasturtium's name comes from the latin nasus (nose) and torquere (to twist), tipping diners off to its fiery, "nose-twisting" flavor.

*W*hen the mad Ophelia of Shakespeare's Hamlet gives pansies to Laertes, she remarks, "And there is pansies, that's for thoughts." The line recalls the origins of the flower's name, which comes from the French pensée, meaning "thought." Its blossom resembles a face frowning as if deep in concentration.

# of Others

BEST KNOWN FOR ITS NARCOTIC QUALITIES, THE POPPY IS ALSO THE FLOWER OF REMEMBRANCE. VETERANS' GROUPS HAVE SOLD PAPER POPPIES SINCE THE FIRST WORLD WAR TO RAISE FUNDS. THE PRACTICE IS PARTICULARLY APT FOR SURVIVORS OF D-DAY, THE ALLIED INVASION OF NORMANDY DURING WORLD WAR II. ARRIVING IN JUNE, 1944, THE TROOPS FOUND THE FRENCH FIELDS BLANKETED WITH THE RED FLOWERS.

THE CHINESE GREW THE DELICIOUSLY SCENTED MAGNOLIA NOT FOR ITS LOVELINESS BUT FOR THE SUPPOSED APHRODISIAC QUALITY OF ITS POWDERED BARK.

IN 1793, WHILE MARIE ANTOINETTE SAT IN PRISON WAITING FOR DEATH, A WOULD-BE RESCUER CONCEALED A MESSAGE IN THE CALYX OF A CARNATION. GAINING ACCESS TO HER CELL, HE DROPPED IT AT HER FEET AS IF BY ACCIDENT. THE QUEEN READ THE MESSAGE BUT DID NOT RECOGNIZE HER SAVIOR. HER JAILERS NOTICED HER AGITATION AND FOILED THE ESCAPE PLOT.

AS JOHANN GOTTFRIED ZINN WANDERED THE MOUNTAINS OF MEXICO IN THE 18TH CENTURY, HE PICKED SOME PURPLE FLOWERS THAT HE HAD NEVER SEEN BEFORE AND PUT THEM IN HIS BAG. WHEN THIEVES LATER ATTACKED HIM, THEY TORE OPEN THE SACK OF WILTED FLOWERS. THEY DECIDED HE WAS A SIMPLETON AND LET HIM GO, CONSIDERING IT BAD LUCK TO HARM THE DULL-WITTED. THE FLOWERS WERE NAMED ZINNIAS AFTER THEIR LUCKY DISCOVERER.

During the Crusades, French King Louis VII adopted the iris as his crest, whereupon it was christened the "Fleur de Louis," or fleur-de-lis. The insignia shows a single upright standard flanked by two drooping falls, representing the three virtues: faith, wisdom, and valor.

Appropriately, the iris takes its name from the Greek goddess of the rainbow. To beckon this goddess, whose duty it was to lead the souls of dead women to paradise, the Greeks planted purple irises on women's graves.

Turkish peasants sometimes constructed the roofs of their dwellings with iris rhizomes. The roots' tight, waterproof quality made them a perfect building material for shelters that could withstand the elements.

Many centuries ago, a famine in Japan prompted the emperor to decree that only edible plants were to be cultivated in gardens. Some quick-thinking Japanese women, who made their face powder from a certain kind of iris root, craftily planted their irises on the thatched roofs of their houses, where the flowers grew --- literally above the law.

Native Americans understood the lethal power of the iris, whose roots contain irisin, a poison. After grinding the iris root, they mixed it with animal bile in the gall bladder of a buffalo. They warmed the mixture over a fire for several days, then dipped their arrow points in it. Even an enemy wounded only slightly with one of these arrows would die within a week.

The Regal IRIS

COMPRISED OF ABOUT 300 SPECIES, THE IRIS FAMILY ENCOMPASSES BOTH BULB AND RHIZOME (UNDERGROUND STEM) ROOT STRUCTURES. WHILE THEIR BLOOMS ARE NOT KNOWN FOR THEIR SCENT, THE ROOTS OF SOME IRISES SMELL LIKE VIOLETS. THE FLOWERS HAVE SIX PETALS— THREE INNER, ERECT PETALS CALLED STANDARDS AND THREE OUTER, DROOPING PETALS CALLED FALLS. THEY COME IN ALMOST EVERY CONCEIVABLE COLOR, EXCEPT RED. BUT ONE VARIETY, THE DULL MAUVE GLADWYN, HAS SEED PODS THAT BURST OPEN IN AUTUMN TO REVEAL A SECRET SPLENDOR OF RUBY-RED SEEDS.

THE SEEDS OF THE IRIS HAVE BEEN USED AS A SUBSTITUTE FOR COFFEE BEANS. AMONG NATIVE AMERICANS, VARIOUS PARTS OF THE PLANT WENT INTO CURES FOR STOMACH ACHES, EAR AND EYE INFECTIONS, AND DYSPEPSIA.

AU BON MARCHE

LE LYS ET LA FLEUR D'ORANGER.

Casa Blanca
Lily

Lilies

Behold the lilies of the field

The genus Lilium consists of about 80 species of lilies, most of which are cultivated as ornamentals. Related to asparagus, yams, garlic, leeks, onions, aloe, and the Hottentot-bread of Africa, these perennials have leafy stems, usually narrow leaves, and a capsule-like fruit containing many seeds. Whether solitary or clustered, a lily's funnel-shaped flowers may be erect, horizontal, or nodding.

Finicky flora: Unlike the bulbs of tulips and daffodils, which are surrounded by water-tight skins, lily bulbs are scaly. Prone to dry out, they won't last long unplanted.

The relaxed petals and conical clusters of the Turk's cap lily make it look like a turban. But don't pick this one for your lapel—it doesn't smell as pleasant as it looks.

According to a Jewish legend, Eve cried after her expulsion from Eden, when she discovered she was pregnant. Lilies grew where the teardrops landed.

Greeks and Romans alike crowned brides with wreaths of lilies and corn, the symbols of virginity and fertility.

Roman Catholics deemed the lily the flower most appropriate for church decoration. To make the blooms truly pure, they removed the stamen and pistils—the sex organs—from each blossom.

In romantic French literature, the lily is the king of flowers and the rose is the queen.

Calla Lily

Functional Flora

Unless made of metal, glass, or stone, almost every place and every thing we use at home, play, work, and worship is directly or indirectly made from plants. Even plastic is derived from oil, the compressed remains of ancient plants and animals (who ate ancient plants).

Where do you hang your hat? In warm climes, people weave, plait, and tie palm fronds and grasses into the walls and roofs of thatched huts. Pueblo Indians mix grass and mud into bricks for their adobe dwellings. Then and now, wilderness lovers have hewn log cabins from timber forests. Lumber also forms the skin and skeleton of colonials and condominiums, Victorians and split-levels, not to mention pavilions, gazebos, pergolas and kiosks.

Large or small, plants can hold it all. Brushes, reeds, withes, saplings, and grasses are woven into baskets, trays, fences, and wicker furniture. Fibers are twisted into rope, and gourds become bottles. And, of course, wood makes everything from corn cribs to coffins, chifforobes to chicken coops, and carts to coasters.

Bedding down with the flora means more than spreading your sleeping bag on the pine needles. Where in the world would we sleep if it weren't for cotton and linen? Futons, pillows, hammocks, and mattresses soften our repose while quilts, blankets, sheets and coverlets warm our toes.

Tools of the trade: starting with spears, bows, and digging sticks, humankind has fashioned countless gadgets and gizmos from plant materials. Pitchforks, water wheels, toothpicks, plows, brooms, mallets, spinning wheels, abacuses, rolling pins, saw horses, paintbrushes, windmills, looms, and chopsticks all have their roots in the plant world.

In the just-plain-fun department, plant matter goes into cuckoo clocks, shadow puppets, baseball bats, jungle gyms, duck decoys, model airplanes, corsages, doll houses, and the Sunday funnies.

The Painter as Naturalist

Art and science have always enjoyed an odd but fulfilling relationship. In their efforts to record their observations, some naturalists have displayed great artistic talent. Likewise, artists hired to illustrate naturalists' findings have sometimes imparted scientific insight. It has been said that without the art of drawing, the development of natural history as we know it today would have been impossible. Yet botanical illustrations of a supposedly documentary nature reveal as much about fashion as they do about science.

The beauty of flowers has motivated all manner of study in all artistic media and endless attempts to preserve forever what is truly ephemeral. Tapestry, textiles, crockery, jewelry, toys, fans, sculpture, and furniture have all celebrated the radiance of flowers.

Flower
Colors

For Roses

Alizarin
Rose Madder   Brilliant
Violet   Parma
Deep Rose

Cadmium
Red Pale   Naples
Yellow   Cadmium
Yellow Pale   Flame
Red

For Violets

Purple
Lake   Brilliant
Violet   Parma
Violet   Parma
Violet with
White

Other Flowers

Marigold
Yellow   Periwinkle
Blue   Geranium

Sap
Green

Mistletoe
Green

Hooker's
Green
No. 1

Forest
Green

Permanent
Green   Deep

Olive
Green

Leaf
Colors

A N APPLE A DAY...

FROM TIME IMMEMORIAL, PEOPLE HAVE RECOGNIZED THE POWER PLANTS HAVE TO HEAL AND SUSTAIN. DEVELOPED BY TRIAL AND ERROR, 85% OF TRADITIONAL HEALTH PRACTICES RELY ON PLANT EXTRACTS. THEIRS IS AN ETHNOPHARMACOPOEIA, STILL THE CURE OF FIRST RESORT FOR 80% OF THE WORLD'S POPULATION.

KEEPERS OF A LONG ORAL HERITAGE, TRADITIONAL HEALERS ARE LIVING LIBRARIES. HIGH-TECH RESEARCHERS HAVE TRANSLATED SOME OF THEIR ANCIENT WISDOM INTO MODERN REMEDIES. TODAY, 121 OF THE MOST FREQUENTLY USED DRUGS, SUCH AS ASPIRIN, ARE DERIVED FROM PLANTS, MANY OF WHICH WERE INTRODUCED TO DOCTORS BY TRADITIONAL HEALERS.

FOXGLOVE

PARTS USED
The Leaves

NAMES
Digitalis
"Folk's glove"

Used for
heart
disease
muscular
dystrophy
narcotic
sedative
sores
tuberculosis
tumors

Used for
cardio-
vascular
disorders
colds
diuretic
epilepsy
fluid
retention
glaucoma

DESCRIPTION

Foxglove is named for its resemblance of its flowers to fingers of the folks gloves. It was described as medically useful as long ago as the first century A.D. The standardized digitalis tablets prescribed today are made from the powdered leaf, and most of the pills are green like the leaves they contain.

Snapdragon Family

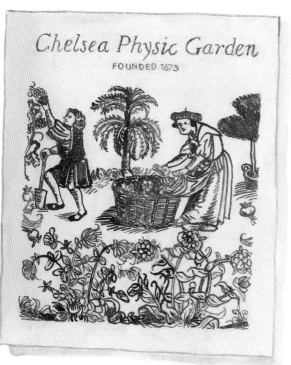

Chelsea Physic Garden
FOUNDED 1673

THE CASE OF THE FOXGLOVE CURE: IN 1775, DOCTOR WILLIAM WITHERING WAS HAVING NO LUCK TREATING DROPSY, THE ABNORMAL ACCUMULATION OF FLUIDS IN THE BODY, WHEN ONE OF HIS PATIENTS MADE A SUDDEN AND UNEXPECTED RECOVERY. BAFFLED, THE DOCTOR CONSULTED THE PATIENT'S FAMILY AND FOUND THEY HAD ADMINISTERED AN HERBAL BREW BASED ON AN OLD FAMILY RECIPE. THE GOOD DOCTOR BEGAN EXPERIMENTING AND SOON IDENTIFIED THE CURATIVE AGENT AS FOXGLOVE, A STALK-LIKE PLANT WITH PURPLE AND PINK FUNNEL-SHAPED FLOWERS. OVER THE NEXT TEN YEARS, WITHERING DOCUMENTED THE SUCCESSFUL TREATMENT OF OVER TWO HUNDRED CASES OF DROPSY AND HEART FAILURE. HE HAD TO EXERCISE GREAT CARE IN DISPENSING THE FOXGLOVE CURE, FOR THE THERAPEUTIC DOSE WAS VERY CLOSE TO THE TOXIC DOSE. SCIENTISTS LATER EXTRACTED TWO CARDIAC GLYCOSIDES, DIGOXIN AND DIGITOXIN, FROM FOXGLOVE. THEY STILL RANK AMONG THE DRUGS MOST EFFECTIVE IN THE TREATMENT OF HEART CONDITIONS.

IMAGINE THE UNDISCOVERED AND UNDOCUMENTED MEDICAL MIRACLES GROWING IN THE WORLD'S RICH BUT THREATENED RAINFORESTS!

MOST FAMILIAR OF THE BULB FLOWERS, THE GENUS TULIPA INCLUDES ABOUT 100 SPECIES OF TULIPS, MOST OF WHICH HAVE A BELL-SHAPED FLOWER AND THICK, BLUISH-GREEN LEAVES CLUSTERED AT THE PLANT'S BASE. AS IN OTHER BULB SPECIES, THE TULIP'S BULB SERVES AS ITS ROOT. A PLANT OF MEDITERRANEAN AND CENTRAL ASIAN ORIGIN, IT HAS ESPECIALLY CLOSE TIES WITH TURKEY. THE PLANT'S NAME COMES FROM THE TURKISH WORD DULBAND, MEANING "TURBAN."

FRENCH BOTANIST CAROLUS CLUSIUS, A PROFESSOR AT LEIDEN UNIVERSITY IN THE 16TH CENTURY, GREW SOME OF HOLLAND'S FIRST TULIPS. IN 1593 HE TRIED TO SELL SOME, BUT HIS ASKING PRICE WAS TOO HIGH. THIEVES THEN STOLE THE BEST SPECIMENS AND SOLD THE SEED.

IN THE 17TH CENTURY, ONE BULB OF SEMPER AUGUSTUS SOLD FOR 5,500 FLORINS, THE EQUIVALENT OF $960. A DUTCH TULIP FARMER WAS SAID TO HAVE CONSUMED A 100,000-FLORIN STEW WHEN HIS COOK MISTOOK SOME OF HIS RAREST BULBS FOR ONIONS. THE COSTLY TULIP WAS CELEBRATED IN THE 18TH-CENTURY COURT OF FRENCH KING LOUIS XV, WHERE LADIES ADORNED THEIR PLUNGING NECKLINES WITH EXPENSIVE VARIETIES.

ONE CANNOT THINK OF THE TULIP WITHOUT THINKING OF HOLLAND. DURING WORLD WAR II, STARVING DUTCH FAMILIES ATE TULIP BULBS TO SURVIVE. TODAY, THE FINEST TULIP GARDEN IN THE WORLD IS KEUKENHOF, NEAR THE DUTCH TOWN OF LISSE.

AMONG THE OTHER BULB FLOWERS IS THE SAFFRON CROCUS, WHOSE HIGHLY PRIZED DRIED STIGMAS ARE USED IN PERFUMES, MEDICINES, DYES, AND FOOD. SAFFRON LENDS FOOD AN INTENSE YELLOW COLOR AND A DISTINCTIVE, SUBTLE FLAVOR.

ONE OF THE FIRST FLOWERS TO EMERGE FROM THE EARTH EACH SPRING, THE BULB-BASED DAFFODIL IS A SYMBOL OF BIRTH AND RENEWAL.

A GREEK MYTH DESCRIBES THE TRAGIC ORIGINS OF THE PURPLE BULB FLOWER CALLED THE HYACINTH. A YOUNG MORTAL BY THAT NAME FELL IN LOVE WITH THE GOD APOLLO, SLIGHTING ANOTHER GOD, ZEPHYRUS. ONE DAY, AS THE LOVERS THREW A DISCUS ABOUT, ZEPHYRUS SWEPT DOWN AND BLEW THE DISCUS INTO HYACINTH'S SKULL. WEEPING OVER HIS DEAD LOVER, APOLLO CREATED THE FLOWER FROM DROPS OF THE YOUTH'S BLOOD.

ulips and other bulbs

ANOTHER GREEK MYTH TELLS HOW THE BULB FLOWER NARCISSUS CAME TO BE. THE NYMPH ECHO FELL IN LOVE WITH A MORTAL NAMED NARCISSUS, WHO DID NOT RETURN HER AFFECTIONS. HEARTBROKEN, ECHO RETIRED TO A CAVE AND DIED THERE. NARCISSUS ALSO DIED, NOT FROM GRIEF BUT FROM VANITY. HE WAS SO ENCHANTED BY HIS REFLECTION IN A POOL OF WATER THAT HE COULD NOT TEAR HIMSELF AWAY. HE LANGUISHED BY THE RIVERBANK AND A FLOWER SPRANG UP WHERE HE DIED.

Floral flights of fancy

"SING TO ME YOUR WORDLESS SONG
O SPIRIT, O BLESSED PARACLETE!
SOOTHE ME TO SLEEP AMONG
THE FLOWERS
WHOSE COLORS ARE COUNTLESS,
WHOSE NAMES ARE UNKNOWN!"

-- BENEDICT WALLET VILAKAZI,
ZULU POET

In TROPICAL ASIA, ELEPHANTS' FEET SCATTER THE TINY SEEDS OF THE PARASITIC RAFFLESIA FLOWER. THE SEEDS BURROW INTO SHALLOW TREE ROOTS AND GERMINATE UNDER THE BARK. STRANGLING THE ROOTS WITH ITS TENDRILS, THE SEEDLING EXTRACTS NOURISHMENT AT THE TREE'S EXPENSE. ITS BUD THEN PIERCES THE BARK AND GROWS TO THE SIZE OF A CABBAGE. WHEN IT BLOOMS, THE NOXIOUS-SMELLING FLOWER DISPLAYS FIVE FLESHY, BOWL-SHAPED LOBES. SOMETIMES REACHING THREE FEET IN DIAMETER, THE RAFFESIA IS THE LARGEST FLOWER IN THE WORLD.

LIKE A HUMMINGBIRD, THE BIRD-OF-PARADISE FLUTTERS AMIDST THE GREEN FOLIAGE OF SOUTH AMERICA. TINTED A BRILLIANT ORANGE AND BLUE, ITS LONG, GRACEFULLY TAPERING SEPALS MAKE THE BLOSSOM RESEMBLE A BIRD IN FLIGHT. BUT IT'S ACTUALLY A MEMBER OF THE BANANA FAMILY.

IT MAY LOOK LIKE ONE, BUT THE BANANA PLANT IS NOT A TREE. CONSTRUCTED OF LAYERS OF CONCENTRIC LEAF BASES, ITS STALK BLOOMS IN A SINGLE HUGE YELLOW-WHITE FLOWER. THE CONE-SHAPED BLOSSOM BECOMES A BUNCH OF BANANAS BEFORE THE STALK DIES. A NEW PURPLE-RINGED STALK THEN GROWS FROM THE SAME PLANT BASE.

GINGER, THE SWEET AND SPICY HALLMARK OF ASIAN CUISINE, COMES FROM THE ROOT OF THE ZINGIBER PLANT. ALTHOUGH NOT AS TASTY, THE SCARLET, PINE CONE-SHAPED FLOWERS OF THE PLANT CAN BE USED AS SOAP IN A PINCH. ITS SUCCULENT SCALES PRODUCE A CLEANSING SAP THAT IMPARTS AN AIR OF SPICY FRESHNESS.

BY NO MEANS MONSTROUS, THE MONSTERA IS A WHITE FLOWER NATIVE TO MEXICO AND GUATEMALA. SURROUNDED BY A PROTECTIVE MANTLE OF PETALS, ITS COB-SHAPED OVARY TAKES AS LONG AS A YEAR TO RIPEN INTO A GREEN FRUIT.

TRUE TO ITS NAME, THE TRAVELER'S PALM PROVIDES RELIEF TO WEARY WANDERERS. REACHING A HEIGHT OF UP TO TWENTY-FIVE FEET, ITS TRUNK ENDS IN A TWO-LAYERED FAN OF LARGE LEAVES. IN THE TREE'S COOLING SHADE, PARCHED VISITORS CAN CUT OPEN THE LOWER LEAF STALKS TO ENJOY A FOUNTAIN OF THIRST-QUENCHING SAP.

ORchIDS

SEX AND THE SINGLE ORCHID

"HARLOTS' FRILLIES IN LAVENDER PLAID,
IRIDESCENT PUCE, AND A BOA
OF PLASHING MAROON DOWN A STEM
ICED WITH GLITTER. WHAT WILL FETCH
THE SILENT EXCLAMATION FROM A BEE?
COME, FRIEND, TORCH YOUR HEELS
WITH MY POLLEN. CARRY ME LIKE A RUMOR
THROUGH THE GREEN TIDES OF YOUR JUNGLE."

"THE ORCHID EXHIBIT," JAGUAR OF
SWEET LAUGHTER, DIANE ACKERMAN, 1991

EACH OF THE 25,000 VARIETIES
OF ORCHIDS IS DISTINGUISHED BY A
FLOWER WITH THREE SEPALS AND
THREE PETALS. FUSED INTO A STALK IN
THE CENTER OF THE FLOWER, AN ORCHID'S
SEXUAL ORGANS ARE KNOWN COLLECTIVELY-
AND SUGGESTIVELY--AS THE COLUMN.

THE NAME ORCHID COMES FROM
THE GREEK WORD FOR TESTICLE. ORCHID
ROOTS, CONSISTING OF A PAIR OF TUBERS,
APPARENTLY REMINDED THE GREEKS... OF
THEIR OWN ROOTS. GREEK WOMEN THOUGHT THEY
COULD CONTROL THE SEX OF THEIR UNBORN CHILDREN WITH ORCHID ROOTS. IF THE FATHER
ATE LARGE, NEW TUBERS, THE CHILD WOULD BE MALE; IF THE MOTHER ATE SMALL, OLD TUBERS,
IT WOULD BE FEMALE. TODAY, SOME SWEAR BY THE APHRODISIAC POWERS OF SALEP, A POWDER
OF GROUND ORCHID TUBERS.

Because they contain no stored food, the orchid's tiny seeds germinate only when penetrated by the threads of a fungus called mycorrhiza. An enzyme in the seed dissolves the fungus, releasing nutrients for the orchid embryo. As soon as the plantlet grows a few green leaves, it can produce its own food.

A highly specialized reproductive device, the orchid is particular about who does its pollinating. Vanilla planifolia, the orchid that produces the vanilla bean, attracts only one kind of bee, the melipone. Its blossom lasts only a single day; if it is not pollinated then, the plant will produce no beans.

Coryanthes macrantha makes a sweet nectar that literally intoxicates bees and other pollinators. As the drunken insects attempt to crawl out of the flower, they stagger into the pollen-coated column. Covered with pollen, they weave on to the next flower.

Lady's Slipper Orchid

The flower of the Ophrys orchid looks, feels, and smells like a female bee of a certain species. Male bees "mate" with the flower, picking up pollen in the process. Then it's on to the next "female," and the cycle begins again.

Say it with Flowers

An anthropological conundrum: If early civilizations arose in hot climates such as the Nile or Euphrates river valleys, why did people start wearing clothes? Possibly to identify their place in society or to protect themselves from the burning sun, insect pests, and other discomforts. Or perhaps they put on clothing as a charm against hostile magic. Amulets hung about the neck warded off the the evil eye.

Gothic folklore suggests wearing garlic amulets to repel vampires.

The most compelling argument for the purpose of human adornment is the pleasure people derive from beauty. To this end, plant materials — leaves, grasses, bamboo, wood, seeds, flowers, and fibers such as cotton and linen — have been skillfully crafted to grace the body.

Aloha! The global tradition of wearing floral wreaths, headdresses, and necklaces manifests itself most perfectly in the Hawaiian art of lei making. Leis are imbued with the spirit of friendship, honor, love, and hospitality.

The first Hawaiians ranked among the most decorated people in the Pacific region. Wearing leis on their heads, necks, shoulders, wrists, and ankles, they danced at ceremonial occasions and strolled through daily life.

Lei makers weave, twist, and braid scores of different and exotic flowers and plants into an almost infinite variety of forms. Proverbs, myths, and local wisdom are entwined with each lei.

The lei hala made from the pandanus fruit is worn at the new year. The hala, a word meaning dead, past, or gone, means the lei should be worn while bidding farewell to old times or places, but not if seeking future luck. Fishermen should not wear a lei hala, for it will bring them bad luck.

"Kauwa ke aloha i na o ka'ana."
   (Love is a slave to the lehua blossom of Ka'ana)

TRADITIONAL HAWAIIAN SAYING

A lei worn for the sacred hula must not be worn for any other purpose, for it belongs to the goddess of the dance.

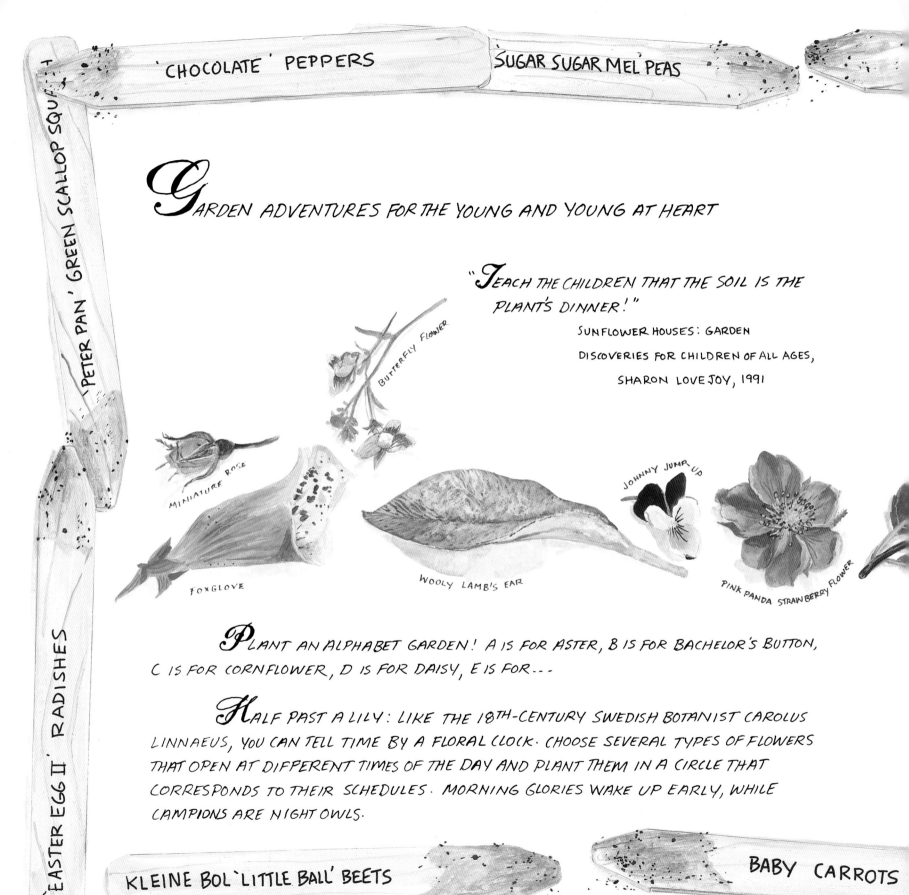

CHOCOLATE PEPPERS

SUGAR SUGAR MEL PEAS

'PETER PAN' GREEN SCALLOP SQUASH

'EASTER EGG II' RADISHES

Garden Adventures for the Young and Young at Heart

"Teach the children that the soil is the plant's dinner!"

Sunflower Houses: Garden Discoveries for Children of all ages, Sharon Lovejoy, 1991

Butterfly Flower

Miniature Rose

Foxglove

Wooly Lamb's Ear

Johnny Jump-Up

Pink Panda Strawberry Flower

Plant an alphabet garden! A is for Aster, B is for Bachelor's Button, C is for Cornflower, D is for Daisy, E is for---

Half past a lily: like the 18th-century Swedish botanist Carolus Linnaeus, you can tell time by a floral clock. Choose several types of flowers that open at different times of the day and plant them in a circle that corresponds to their schedules. Morning glories wake up early, while campions are night owls.

KLEINE BOL 'LITTLE BALL' BEETS

BABY CARROTS

'TOM THUMB' LETTUCE

'SUGAR BABY' WATERMELONS

'RUBY PEARL' CHERRY TOMATOES

'BABY BOO' MINI PUMPKIN

Message in a bottle: without picking it off its stalk, scratch a message or draw a little boat on a newly formed cucumber or zucchini and gently slip it inside a clear, narrow-necked glass bottle. Check its progress each day as it grows and watch the boat turn into a ship.

Harold, eat your vegetables! After picking fast-growing radishes from your garden, trim off their roots and leaves and slice them into thin disks. Make a cut to the center of each disk and assemble into radish jacks. Or, you can play marbles with whole ones. If you grow carrots, you can pick the pretty blossoms; zucchini from your vegetable patch can be cut into cheerful daisies. You can also have fun with home-grown cucumbers: hollow out some slices and make a cuke chain.

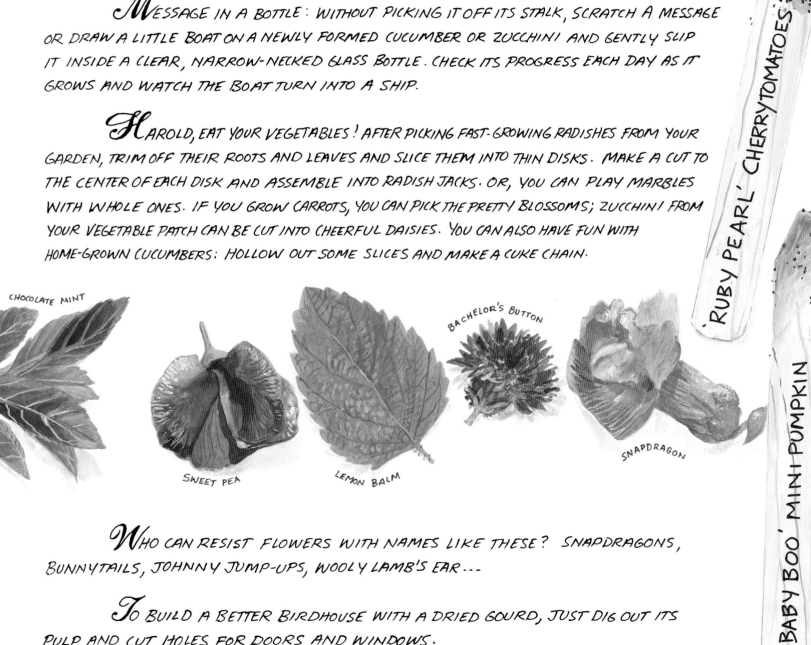

CHOCOLATE MINT

SWEET PEA

LEMON BALM

BACHELOR'S BUTTON

SNAPDRAGON

Who can resist flowers with names like these? Snapdragons, bunnytails, johnny jump-ups, wooly lamb's ear...

To build a better birdhouse with a dried gourd, just dig out its pulp and cut holes for doors and windows.

PLANET'

BABY EGGPLANT 'LITTLE FINGERS'

MINI CORN 'PINK BO PEEP'

"Et les fruits passeront la promesse des fleurs."

(And the fruits will outdo what the flowers have promised.)

PRIÈRE POUR LE ROI HENRI LE GRAND
(PRAYER FOR KING HENRI THE GREAT),
HENRI IV
FRANCOIS DE MALHERBE, 1605

Fruit Salad

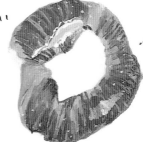

"Outside the courtyard but stretching close lies a large orchard of four acres, where the apple with its glossy burden, the sweet fig

VEGETABLES COME FROM THE ROOTS, STEMS, AND LEAVES OF THE PLANT, BUT FRUIT HAS ONLY ONE SOURCE: IT IS THE PLANT'S OVARY. SOME "VEGETABLES," SUCH AS TOMATOES AND AVOCADOS, ARE ACTUALLY FRUITS. CONVERSELY, SOME MELONS ARE VEGETABLES. OUR SWEET-TOOTH SEEMS TO OVERRIDE SCIENCE WHEN WE DECIDE WHAT WE'RE EATING.

OUR LANGUAGE IS SWEETENED BY FRUITY IDIOMS. A SUCCESSFUL ENDEAVOR IS FRUITFUL, WHILE ONE THAT FAILS IS FRUITLESS. OUR EFFORTS PAY OFF WHEN THEY BEAR FRUIT OR COME TO FRUITION.

GENETICALLY, THE PLUM IS REALLY A GIANT CHERRY. THE MOST FREQUENTLY EATEN VARIETY TODAY, THE EGG-SIZED GREENGAGE PLUM EVOKED THE DESCRIPTIVE POWERS OF EDWARD BUNYARD, A 20TH-CENTURY ENGLISH NURSERYMAN:

"IT [HAS A] CLEAR, TRANSPARENT LOOK; A SLIGHT FLUSH OF RED AND THEN ONE LOOKS INTO THE DEPTHS OF TRANSPARENT AMBER AS ONE LOOKS INTO AN OPAL, UNCERTAIN HOW FAR THE EYE CAN PENETRATE."

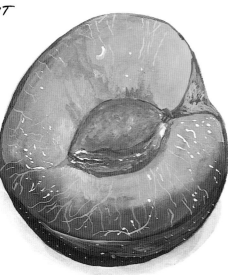

up to the gates, and with a hedge running down on either side, trees hang their greenery on high, the pear and the pomegranate, and the luxuriant olive." —THE ODYSSEY, HOMER, C. 9TH CENTURY B.C.

WHETHER SWEET, SOUR, OR BITTER, THE CHERRY DERIVES ITS NAME FROM THE GREEK DESIGNATION, KERASOS. SUGARY MARASCHINO CHERRIES OF SHIRLEY TEMPLE FAME START OUT AS VERY SOUR FRUIT. AFTER PITTING AND BLEACHING THE CHERRIES, PROCESSORS ADD SYRUP, BITTER ALMOND OIL, AND RED OR GREEN COLORING.

OF CHINESE ORIGIN, THE VELVETY PEACH IS LADEN WITH EROTIC METAPHOR. ITS SKIN FEELS STARTLINGLY LIKE HUMAN SKIN.

TO REPRODUCE MOST SUCCESSFULLY, AN APPLE TREE SHOULD GENERATE MANY SMALL FRUITS RATHER THAN A FEW LARGE ONES. ANCIENT FARMERS BRED THE TREE AWAY FROM ITS NATURAL HABITS, FORCING IT TO YIELD THE LARGE, SWEET-TART FRUIT KNOWN TODAY.

IN THE UNITED STATES, COMMUNITIES ONCE GATHERED FOR "PARING BEES," IN WHICH THEY PEELED APPLES TO BE DRIED AND STORED FOR FUTURE USE. GIRLS THREW THE LONG SPIRALS OF APPLE SKIN OVER THEIR SHOULDERS, HOPING TO SEE THE SHAPE OF THEIR FUTURE HUSBANDS' INITIALS IN THE DISCARDED PEEL.

Berries

Berry Delicious

"There's a berry which makes my pony's bed;
And another one which is green when red;
And there's one which rubs you all the wrong way;
And another which swims and quacks all day;
There's one you can play, to beguile your care;
And one at their necks the ladies wear;
There's a berry which seems to be much depressed;
And one is a bird with a speckled breast;
There's one we can see when the tide is low,
And the last you will be when older you grow."

(The answers to the riddle are: strawberry, blackberry, raspberry, gooseberry, checkerberry, mulberry, blueberry, partridge-berry, barberry, elderberry.)

Sunflower Houses, Sharon Lovejoy, 1991

Botanists refer to the strawberry as a false or accessory fruit. The seeds that dot the outside of the red berry are the real thing, while the juicy red flesh is merely a receptacle.

Black Currant   Red Currant   Wild Strawberry   Black Mulberry

Red Raspberry

*T*HE RICE WINE COLOR WE ASSOCIATE WITH RIPE RASPBERRIES IS BUT ONE OF THE SHADES THIS PIQUANT FRUIT DISPLAYS. THE COLOR OF RASPBERRIES RUNS THE GAMUT FROM WHITE TO BLACK, WITH YELLOW, ORANGE, PINK, RED, AND PURPLE VERSIONS IN BETWEEN. THE BERRY'S NAME MOST LIKELY COMES FROM THE OLD ENGLISH RASPIS, WHICH DESCRIBES ITS SLIGHTLY FUZZY OR "RASPING" SURFACE.

*A*S DELICIOUS AS ITS ETHEREAL NAME SUGGESTS, THE GOLDEN CLOUDBERRY THRIVES IN NORTHERN SCANDINAVIA WHERE THE BORDERS OF NORWAY, SWEDEN, AND FINLAND MEET. THE OTHERWISE PEACEFUL COUNTRIES HAVE BEEN KNOWN TO ENGAGE IN "CLOUDBERRY WARS" OVER THE REGION WHERE THE SUMPTUOUS FRUIT GROWS. TO KEEP THE PEACE, THE SWEDISH MINISTRY FOR FOREIGN AFFAIRS ONCE MAINTAINED A SPECIAL SECTION FOR CLOUDBERRY DIPLOMACY.

*I*N BRITAIN, AN UNWANTED THIRD PERSON AT A LOVERS' MEETING IS CALLED A GOOSEBERRY. THIS SMALL, GLOBE-SHAPED FRUIT IS SO NAMED BECAUSE ITS FLAVOR GOES WELL WITH OILY MEATS SUCH AS GOOSE.

*T*HE TART CRANBERRY IS PROBABLY BEST KNOWN IN THE FORM OF SAUCE AT THE THANKSGIVING TABLE. CRANBERRY FARMERS USED TO SORT THE FRUIT BY POURING IT IN QUANTITY DOWN A FLIGHT OF STAIRS. THE INTACT BERRIES BOUNCED AND ROLLED TO THE BOTTOM, WHILE THE DAMAGED SPECIMENS LOLLED ON THE STEPS. MODERN CRANBERRY-SORTING MACHINES STILL EMPLOY THIS PRINCIPLE.

Blueberry

Raspberry

White Gooseberry

Red Gooseberry

Blackberry

Strawberry

Tangy Citrus Trivia

In days gone by, fashionable European and American hosts sometimes placed kumquat trees on the table so guests could pick the fruit. Although it looks like a miniature orange, the kumquat does not have a golden flavor. Unless prepared with syrup or sugar, they deliver a sour, face-scrunching punch.

The luscious flavor of the orange tree's fruit pales in comparison to the heady fragrance of its blossoms. An evening stroll through a flowering orange grove is a voyage to a sweet and spicy land where the breeze carries clouds of almost sinful pleasure.

Discovered by Anna-Marie de Nerola, an Italian princess, neroli oil is extracted from bitter orange blossoms. The princess used the extremely expensive essence to scent her gloves. The oil also has antidepressant qualities.

A Canton orange known as the bergamot is the secret behind Earl Grey tea. When mixed with China or Darjeeling tea, its oil imparts the distinctive Earl Grey flavor. The tea is named for the British prime minister who popularized it in England after an 1830 visit to China.

ENGLISH SUBJECTS, SPECIFICALLY ENGLISH SAILORS, ARE SOMETIMES REFERRED TO AS "LIMEY." USUALLY CONSIDERED DEROGATORY, THE TERM HAS ITS ROOTS IN THE SAILORS' PRACTICE OF DRINKING LIME JUICE TO AVOID GETTING SCURVY. THE LIME'S VITAMIN C CONTENT HELPED PREVENT THE DISEASE. A TROPICAL RELATIVE OF THE SUB-TROPICAL LEMON, THE LIME AND ITS COUSIN ARE OFTEN SQUEEZED OVER TROPICAL FRUITS SUCH AS PAPAYA, GUAVA, AND AVOCADO TO GIVE THEM EXTRA ZIP.

THE YUZU, A CITRUS FRUIT OF TIBET, BEARS ITS FRUIT IN LATE AUTUMN. ON THE EVENING OF THE WINTER SOLSTICE, THE JAPANESE WRAP THE SMALL, GOLDEN FRUITS IN CHEESECLOTH AND FLOAT THEIR LETTING THEM IN BATHS, THE YUZU-SCENTED STEAM WASH OVER THEM.

GRAPEFRUITS GROW IN CLUSTERS. PERHAPS THIS GRAPE-LIKE TENDENCY GAVE THE GRAPEFRUIT ITS NAME.

Exotic Fruits

Most people know the carambola by its popular name, starfruit. When sliced, the Indonesian fruit presents a star-shaped cross-section of mild-flavored, juicy flesh. Starfruit slices add a whimsical touch to fruit salad.

The lychee, or litchi, is a small, round tropical fruit native to China and Southeast Asia. Its knobby red skin turns brown during shipment abroad, but its flesh retains a pale pink blush and the flavor of a perfumed grape.

A native of the Southeast Asian rainforest, the durian is a large green fruit with a spiky shell. When ripe, the fruit has a strong odor that has been compared to civet cat, sewage, onions, and over-ripe cheese. Carrying it on public transportation is therefore forbidden in Indonesia and Japan. Still, its fans vigorously defend its custardy flavor. In 1973, the journal Horticulture begged to differ, publishing this poem:

> The durian neither Wallace nor Darwin agreed on it.
> Darwin said: "May your worst enemies be forced to feed on it."
> Wallace cried "it's delicious", Darwin replied "I'm suspicious,
> for the flavor is scented like papaya fermented,
> after a fruit-eating bat has peed on it."

The jackfruit of Southeast Asia can grow as large as 90 pounds. Surrounded by green, spiky skin, its pale yellow flesh tastes like bananas and is peppered with as many as 500 edible seeds, which are sometimes referred to as breadnuts.

A persnickety Vietnamese tree called the mangosteen produces a small, purple-skinned fruit with delicate white sections of flesh. The fruit has the texture of a well-ripened plum and the flavor of an apple.

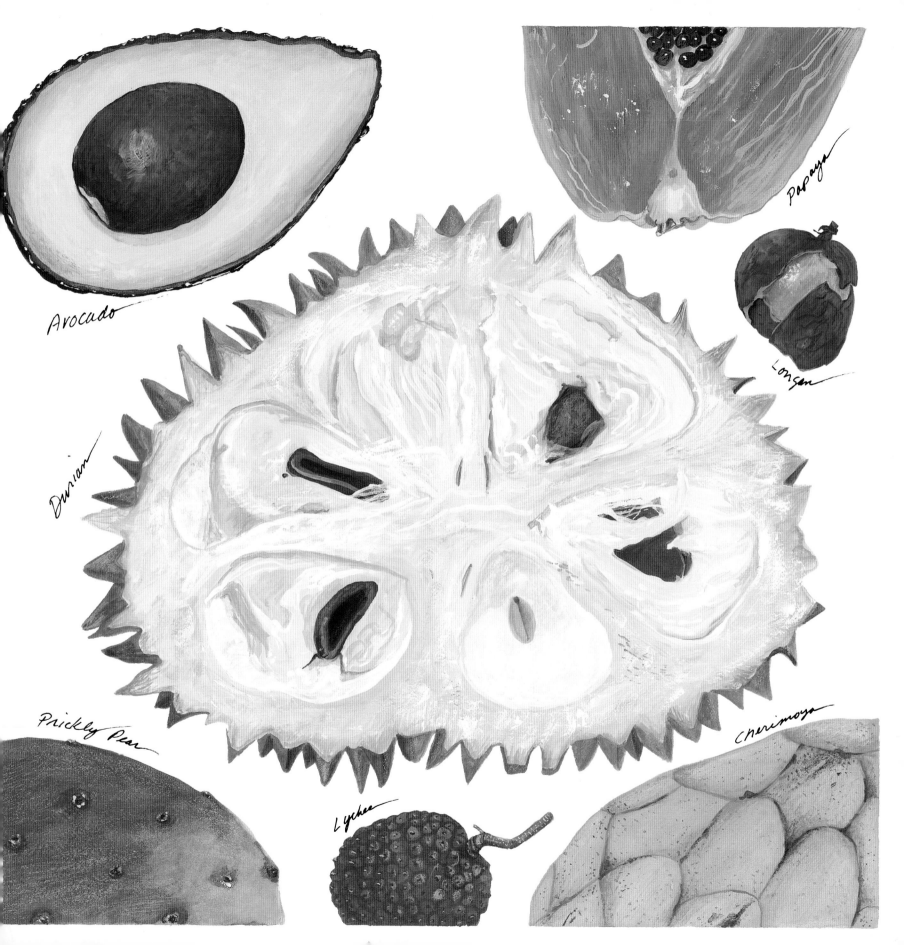

Avocado

Papaya

Longan

Durian

Prickly Pear

Lychee

Cherimoya

GRAPES

"IN VINO VERITAS"

IN WINE IS TRUTH

— PLINY THE ELDER, 1ST CENTURY A·D·

Viticulture, the art of grape cultivation, is nearly as old as civilization itself. In Egyptian tomb paintings dating from the 8th century B·C·, arched and trellised vines are laden with an abundance of purple grapes, which gardeners collect with awed expressions.

THE FRUIT OF THE VINE

*P*HOENICIAN TRADERS CARRIED THE CLIMBING, WOODY VINE TO FRANCE IN THE 6TH CENTURY B.C.; ROMAN CONQUERORS LATER BROUGHT GRAPES TO THE RHINE VALLEY OF GERMANY. IN THE 2ND CENTURY B.C., PLINY THE ELDER DESCRIBED MORE THAN 91 JUICY VARIETIES OF GRAPES AND AT LEAST 50 KINDS OF WINE. OF THE ESTIMATED 10,000 GRAPE VARIETIES KNOWN TODAY, ONLY A DOZEN OR SO DELIVER VOLUPTUOUS BUNCHES OF FRUIT TO THE TABLE.

*I*N THE LATE 19TH CENTURY, VINTNERS BROUGHT NORTH AMERICAN GRAPEVINES TO EUROPE, CURIOUS TO SEE WHAT SUBTLETIES OF BOUQUET OR FLAVOR THE UNFAMILIAR SPECIES MIGHT ADD TO THEIR WINE. THEIR FASCINATION TURNED TO HORROR WHEN A STOWAWAY PARASITE BEGAN TO WREAK HAVOC. PHYLLOXERA, A VINE LOUSE NATIVE TO EASTERN NORTH AMERICA, DESTROYED VINEYARDS ACROSS EUROPE AT A TERRIFYING SPEED. THE NIGHTMARE FINALLY ENDED AFTER ALMOST TWENTY YEARS, WHEN VINTNERS SUCCEEDED IN GRAFTING ROOTS FROM RESISTANT NORTH AMERICAN STRAINS TO EUROPEAN VINES.

Nicoise

Atalanti

Kalamata

Greek Green

Napoleon

Greek oil-cured

Bella Cerignola

French oil-cured

Apulian

A CRADLE OF CULTIVATION

"... AND THERE WERE FIGS AND VINES, AND ITS WINE WAS MORE PLENTIFUL THAN WATER. ITS HONEY WAS IN ABUNDANCE AND ITS OIL MAGNIFICENT. EVERY FRUIT GREW ON ITS TREES AND ITS BARLEY AND WHEAT WERE BEYOND MEASURE."

— SINUHE, EGYPTIAN, 20TH CENTURY B.C.

KNOWN AS ONE OF THE CRADLES OF CIVILIZATION, THE MEDITERRANEAN REGION WAS ALSO THE CRADLE OF CULTIVATION. AS IN ANCIENT DAYS, ITS PEOPLE STILL LIVE ON OLIVES, FIGS, DATES, AND POMEGRANATES AND THE SAVORY OILS, SYRUPS, AND LIQUORS THEY YIELD. THEIR MERE SCENT OR FLAVOR CAN TRANSPORT US TO THE DESERT, WHERE OLIVE TREES CROUCH ON GNARLED TRUNKS, AND STATELY DATE PALMS SWAY IN THE BREEZE.

IN THE DESERT, THE DATE IS THE STAFF OF LIFE. BEDOUINS, THE NOMADIC DENIZENS OF THE NEGEV, CAN EXIST FOR LONG PERIODS ON ALMOST NOTHING BUT DRIED DATES AND MILK. EACH DATE PALM HAS EITHER MALE OR FEMALE FLOWERS, NOT BOTH. BECAUSE THE SEEDLESS FRUIT FROM UNPOLLINATED FLOWERS IS INFERIOR, FARMERS TIE BRANCHES OF MALE FLOWERS ONTO FEMALE TREES TO FOSTER FERTILIZATION.

Lebanese Black

Cracked Provençal

Greek Black

Lebanese Green

Gaeta

Arbequina   Nyons   Syrian   Moroccan Oil-cured

Jordanian Almeja

Sicilian Oil-cured

Algerian

THE FIG AS WE KNOW IT IS NOT A TRUE FRUIT, BUT A RECEPTACLE CALLED A SYCONIUM, LINED WITH MANY TINY FLOWERS THAT BECOME TINY FRUITS. A MINISCULE FIG WASP LIVES INSIDE THE SYCONIUM OF SOME FIG VARIETIES AND ACTS AS THE POLLINATOR.

GREEK MYTH TELLS OF DEMETER, GODDESS OF THE HARVEST, WHOSE BEAUTIFUL DAUGHTER PERSEPHONE WAS KIDNAPPED BY HADES, THE UNDERWORLD GOD. PERSEPHONE VOWED NOT TO EAT IN CAPTIVITY, BUT SHE SUCCUMBED TO THE JEWELED FRUIT OF THE POMEGRANATE, SWALLOWING SIX SEEDS. HADES FINALLY FREED HER ON THE CONDITION THAT SHE RETURN TO THE UNDERWORLD FOR SIX MONTHS EACH YEAR, ONE FOR EVERY SEED SHE HAD SWALLOWED. DEMETER'S ANNUAL GRIEF DURING THIS TIME GAVE BIRTH TO THE COLD, DARK WINTER MONTHS.

BECAUSE OF THEIR BITTERNESS, OLIVES CANNOT BE EATEN OFF THE TREE; THEY MUST BE CURED WITH POTASH OR LYE AND THEN PICKLED IN SALT. THE FRUIT OF THE OLIVE TREE YIELDS A DELIGHTFUL COOKING OIL THAT CAN ALSO FUEL LAMPS, SOOTHE ILLNESS, AND ENHANCE A MASSAGE.

"WHEN I WAS A CHILD, MY BROTHERS AND I WERE ALLOWED TO JOIN THE FARMERS IN THE OLIVE GATHERING ON THE GROUNDS OF THE VILLA. OUR JOB WAS TO COLLECT THE FRUIT THAT FELL BY ACCIDENT FROM THE BASKETS HELD BY THOSE PICKING FROM THE BRANCHES UP HIGH. HOW WE LOOKED FORWARD TO THE DAY WHEN WE MIGHT BE ALLOWED TO CLIMB THOSE TREES OURSELVES."

FOODS OF ITALY, GUILIANO BUGIALLI, 1984

Calamata Green

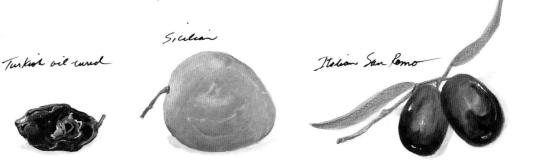

manzanilla   French Picholine   Turkish oil-cured   Sicilian   Italian San Remo

Apple

Horned Melon

Plum

Red currant

Cherry

Black currant

Rose hips

Banana

Lime

Grapes

Cherimoya

Papaya

Strawberry

Fig

Red Gooseberry

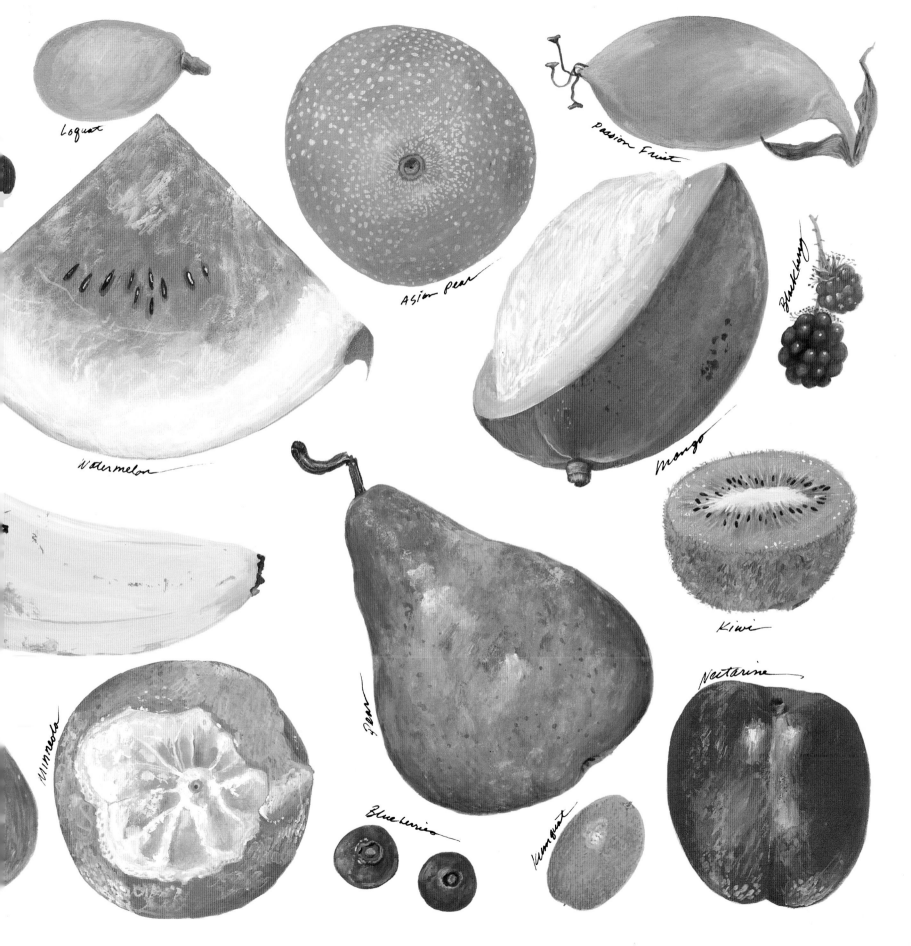

Loquat

Asian Pear

Passion Fruit

Blackberry

Watermelon

Mango

Kiwi

Pear

Nectarine

Minneola

Blueberries

Kumquat

Black Jack Oak

Bur Oak

Chestnut Oak

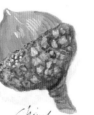

Interior Live Oak

With great joy and deep reverence for Mother Earth and her miraculous botanical cloak.

THANK YOU TO THE WONDERFUL INDIVIDUALS AND ORGANIZATIONS WHO CONTINUE TO ENRICH MY WORK ON THESE BOOKS! ...

TO MY CREATIVE PARTNER AND DEAR FRIEND KRISTIN JOYCE, WHO NURTURES OUR RELATIONSHIP AND THESE SWANS ISLAND BOOKS LIKE TENDER FLOWERS. MAY HER FAMILY, AND ESPECIALLY HER SUPPORTIVE HUSBAND DON -- WHO LENDS US HUNDREDS OF BOOKS -- FLOURISH WITH AS MUCH LOVE AND CARE.

TO WRITER SHELLEI ADDISON OF FLYING FISH BOOKS FOR ONCE AGAIN CONTRIBUTING INVALUABLE RESEARCH AND LOVELY TEXT. A ROSE INDEED!

Red Oak

Bear Oak

TO CONSTANCE JONES, LINE EDITOR EXTRAORDINAIRE.

California White Oak

TO JULIE NATHAN FOR HER DELIGHTFUL NATURE AND HER CLEVER AND CONSTANT HELP.

TO OUR FORMER PUBLISHER, THE DELIGHTFUL JENNY BARRY OF COLLINS PUBLISHERS SAN FRANCISCO, AND TO HER GREAT STAFF.

Scarlet Oak

Shingle Oak

TO OUR EXCITING, NEW HOME WITH SMITHMARK PUBLISHERS AND TO THE CONTAGIOUS ENTHUSIASM OF OUR NEW PUBLISHER, MARTA HALLETT AND HER WONDERFUL EXECUTIVE EDITOR, ELIZABETH SULLIVAN.

TO MY THREE CHILDREN, WENDY, SUNNY, AND JONATHAN, FOR THEIR LOVE, ENCOURAGEMENT, AND CREATIVE HELP. TO MY FATHER-IN-LAW, DR. BERNARD KOCH, AND TO ALL MY TREASURED FAMILY AND FRIENDS.

ALSO TO MY DEAR SISTER DIANE AND TO HER HUSBAND, GARY MEEHAN OF BONNY DOON FARM.

TO MY DEAR BROTHER HANK MOELLER AND SISTER-IN-LAW, LANA HOPE, FOR CAREFULLY TENDING OUR PARENTS' GARDENS AND FOR ALL THEIR HELP WITH COLLECTING THE GREENS AND FLOWERS USED THROUGHOUT THIS BOOK.

TO THE CALIFORNIA ACADEMY OF SCIENCES IN SAN FRANCISCO FOR THEIR IMPRESSIVE BIODIVERSITY RESOURCE CENTER, KNOWN FOR ONE OF THE LARGEST COLLECTIONS OF INFORMATION OF ITS KIND IN THE UNITED STATES. TO ITS HELPFUL COORDINATOR ANNE MALLEY AND HER COLLEAGUE FRANK ALMEADA, BOTANIST, CURATOR, AND COORDINATOR OF THE CAS BOTANICAL LIBRARY.

TO SUE MINTER, CURATOR OF THE VENERABLE CHELSEA PHYSIC GARDEN IN LONDON, FOR A SPLENDID PRIVATE VISIT AND FOR ENHANCING MY VIEW OF HOMEOPATHIC MEDICINE, IN PARTICULAR.

TO THREE OTHER EQUALLY INSPIRING AND FAVORITE ENGLISH SITES--THE HISTORY OF GARDENING MUSEUM, THE ROYAL BOTANIC GARDENS AT KEW, AND THE BRITISH MUSEUM OF NATURAL HISTORY FOR EACH ENRICHING MY WORLD VIEW OF BOTANY IN VARIOUS WAYS.

Pin Oak

TO SYLVIA A. EARLE FOR HER INCREDIBLE COLLECTION OF MARINE PLANTS AND FOR HER LIFE'S WORK DEVOTED TO PRESERVING THE EXQUISITE MEADOWS OF THE DEEP.

TO THE FRENCH ENTOMOLOGIST J.H. FABRE FOR HIS DEVOTED LOVE OF "BUGS" AND FOR REVEALING THEIR ESSENTIAL CONNECTION TO BOTANY—PROVOCATION ENOUGH TO PROMPT OUR FOURTH BOOK IN THIS SERIES!

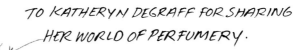

Southern Overcup Oak

TO KATHERYN DEGRAFF FOR SHARING HER WORLD OF PERFUMERY.

Post Oak

TO BEATRIX POTTER AND J.J. GRANDVILLE FOR THEIR INSPIRED AND BEAUTIFUL WORKS.

Selected Glossary

ANGIOSPERMS - FLOWERING SEED PLANTS.

CHLOROPHYLL - CHEMICAL SUBSTANCE WHICH ABSORBS SUNLIGHT AND STORES IT AS ENERGY FOR FUTURE USE BY PLANTS.

COMPOUND INFLORESCENCE - A FLOWER BLOSSOM MADE UP OF HUNDREDS OF "FLORETS." EACH FLORET HAS ITS OWN OVARY, STIGMA, STYLE, AND ANTHERS AND PRODUCES A SINGLE SEED.

DRYLANDS - HABITATS, INCLUDING DESERTS AND POLAR REGIONS, CHARACTERIZED BY THE ABSENCE OF RAIN OR USABLE PRECIPITATION.

GYMNOSPERMS - NON-FLOWERING SEED PLANTS.

HYPHAE - THE INTERCONNECTED FILAMENTS WHICH FORM THE ROOT STRUCTURE OF MUSHROOMS.

LENTICELS - AIR HOLES IN TREE BARK WHICH ALLOW THE TREE TO BREATHE.

PHOTOSYNTHESIS - COMPLEX PROCESS BY WHICH PLANTS CONVERT SUNLIGHT INTO THEIR FOOD.

PISTIL (OR CARPEL) - THE FEMALE REPRODUCTIVE ORGAN OF A FLOWER. IT CONSISTS OF A STICKY STIGMA WHICH TRAPS POLLEN GRAINS, AN OVARY WHICH HOLDS THE FLOWER'S EGGS, AND A STYLE, THE TUBE WHICH POLLEN TRAVELS DOWN TO FERTILIZE THE EGG CELLS.

RHIZOMES - UNDERGROUND HORIZONTAL STEMS THAT CAN TAKE ROOT AND PRODUCE NEW PLANTS.

SPORE - SINGLE CELLS CONTAINING THE GENETIC BLUEPRINT OF A PLANT WHICH ARE RELEASED INSTEAD OF SEEDS BY NON-FLOWERING PLANTS. THESE PLANTS PRODUCE MILLIONS OF SPORES TO INCREASE THEIR SLIM ODDS OF SURVIVAL.

STAMEN - THE MALE REPRODUCTIVE ORGAN OF A FLOWER. EACH STAMEN SUPPORTS SACK-LIKE ANTHERS WHICH STORE THE PLANT'S POLLEN GRAINS.

VITICULTURE - THE ART OF GRAPE CULTIVATION.

WETLANDS - HABITATS INCLUDING MARSHES, BOGS, FENS, SWAMPS, MIRES, SALTMARSHES, MANGROVE SWAMPS, ESTUARIES, PRAIRIE POTHOLES, LAKES, AND RIVERS CHARACTERIZED BY A HIGH PERCENTAGE OF SOIL MOISTURE.

Printed in Hong Kong by
Hong Kong Graphic and Printing Ltd.